THE GUNGE FILE

EPISODES IN THE LIFE OF RAY GUNGE
SELF-STYLED CATERING WIZARD OF
THE NORTH

BY
DEREK COOPER

ILLUSTRATED BY
BILL TIDY

Routledge & Kegan Paul
London

First published in 1986 by
Routledge & Kegan Paul Ltd
11 New Fetter Lane, London EC4P 4EE

Set in 11/14 Bembo
by Columns of Reading
and printed in Great Britain
by T.J. Press (Padstow) Ltd
Padstow, Cornwall

British Library Cataloguing in Publication Data
Cooper, Derek
The Gunge file: episodes in the life of Ray
Gunge, self-styled catering wizard of the north.
1. Caterers and catering.—Great Britain.—Anecdotes,
facetiae, satire, etc.
I. Title
338.4'7647   9541'0207   TX910.G7
ISBN 0-7102-1045-0

CONTENTS

FOREWORD BY RAY GUNGE B.E.M., F.B.C.C.*

It is fashionable among some members of the press to deride our traditional cuisine and hold it up to public ridicule. But, as has been truly said, a nation marches on its stomach and by its stomach be it known. Show me your stomach, as Brillat-Savarin so sagely put it, and I will show you what I have eaten.

Like others who have climbed slowly but surely to the top of their professional tree I have in my time been exposed to criticism from the ill-informed and envious. But I can truly say that it is with a deep sense of humility that I give my imprimatur to this little book in the hope that those who come after will do as well. A man has to cook what he has to cook, whatever it may be and wherever it may be.

Ray Gunge
Hardtack Hall
Noshleigh

*Fellow of the British Caterers Council

INTRODUCTION

Some of this material was originally published in the *Listener*, the *Guardian*, the *Observer* and *World Medicine*. However it was in the pages of the *Catering Times* that Ray Gunge made his first explosive appearance. I am grateful to its editor Miles Quest for sticking his journalistic neck out so recklessly. Gunge has always been surrounded by controversy. Difficult, testy, unpredictable, he remains very much a man of his time, never afraid, as he vividly puts it, to put his fork where his mouth is.

In 1975 a small group of his supporters formed the Friends of Gunge and in the following year, fearful that the self-styled Catering Wizard of the North might fade away through neglect, they decreed him to be a Listed Person. Gunge, with characteristic modesty, remains detached from what over the years has become a cult following. 'If I have been a catering catalyst', he once said to me, 'so be it. It's no good burying your undoubted talents under a brick wall.'

At the request of the Ancient Guild of Sandwich-makers part of the proceeds of this book will pay for the execution of a tasteful stained-glass window in Snackwrights Hall commemorating various episodes in the career of the maestro. He will be shown ascending in a candyfloss cloud to the great washing-up area in the sky leaving lesser figures in the world of snackdom far behind. The working drawings for this major work of vitreous art have been pronounced by Gunge to be 'highly appropriate'.

Derek Cooper

FROGS LEGS
AND FANCY KNICKERS

This record of a very kind and gentle catering giant might just as well begin at the beginning. As Gunge himself would say: Start As You Mean To Go On!

It was Eric D. Croft, former director of the forward-looking British Hotels and Restaurants Association, who first brought us together. In 1966 when I was writing the *Bad Food Guide*, I sought audience of him to discuss why eating out in Britain enjoyed such a poor reputation. 'Eating in Britain', he wrote back, 'does not enjoy a poor reputation.' And that was that. I never did get to see Mr Croft but now and again he would pop up in the papers defending his fellow caterers.

Towards the end of 1970 Mr Croft was interviewed for the BBC by Frank Hennig. There had been criticisms of our food by foreign visitors, particularly the French. Frank suggested to Mr Croft that although you could usually get a good meal in a small French town you couldn't always get a good meal in a small English town. It seemed an acceptable and unexceptionable statement of fact.

But Mr Croft wasn't having any: 'I would say you can be pretty sure in France that you *wouldn't* get a good meal!' He went on to explain to the bewildered Frank that, for a start, there was no basically good food in France anyway.

'What do you get? Veal! You don't get a decent piece of ham, you don't get any beef. You don't get any fish that's worthwhile – the only thing you've probably eaten in France is sauces and they *have* to make damn good sauces because the food isn't as good basically as the food you've got in this country.'

There was plenty more in the same challenging vein and it certainly made good copy. So good that the following day I had a phone call from BBC Radio Noshleigh asking me if I would engage in public debate with Ray Gunge on the question of eating out in Britain.

The name of course I had heard before and I knew too that Gunge had always been a scourge of those who belittle our gastronomic heritage. 'British food', he had said on platforms throughout the country, 'is *nullus secundus* and definitely tops.'

A former Grand Master of the Guild of Sandwichmakers, Gunge was still chairman of the aggressively forward-looking British Caterers Council and was always available for a quote. Only the week before the *Observer* had reprinted his definitive dictum on motorway catering in their *Sayings of the Week* column. 'It is better', Gunge had pronounced when speaking *ex cathedra* at a formal

High Tea in Snackmakers Hall, 'to travel hopefully than to stop.' And I recall a typically abrasive comment at the time of the newspaper exposés of restaurant kitchens deep in mouse droppings: '*Mouse* droppings, sir! If they'd found *elephant* droppings the story might have had some point. A kitchen without mouse droppings is like a pub without a dartboard; an abomination, sir!'

So, a formidable adversary. And as it turned out not one with whom even Brian Redhead could get more than half a word in edgeways. I made my way down to the basement of Broadcasting House to studio B15 where a line had been booked to BBC Radio Noshleigh. Putting the headphones on I heard for the first time the booming and inimitable voice of Gunge, a voice I was to become familiar with over the years.

'Could you get me a cup of tea, lad, I feel a bit throaty.' Then, unaware of my presence in the London studio, he told the producer that he felt I shouldn't have been invited to take part in the programme at all. 'A bit of a troublemaker. I can't stand these people who keep knocking our old country. Quislings, I'd say.'

I coughed discreetly. The studio manager in Noshleigh heard but not Gunge. 'Could you put your cans on, Mr Gunge, I think we've got contact with London.'

'Cans, dear boy? I haven't got any cans. Cans of what? Cat food?' And Gunge gave a merry chuckle. 'It's not all cans you know, you're a bit out of touch with what's going on!'

'The headphones,' I heard the studio manager explain, 'if you put them on I think you'll be able to talk to Derek Cooper.'

'Oh, these! You should have said. Hallo, are you there Mr Cooper?'

And so I established verbal contact for the first time with the grand old man of British catering. In those days I was writing a column for the *Guardian* on food and now and again I would take a swipe at some eccentricity of the catering scene.

'I see your stuff, Mr Cooper. With due respect, I think you're doing our country a great disservice but then that's your privilege.'

We were off to a good start.

The producer sent me a transcript of our conversation; although, come to think of it, conversation has never been Gunge's forte. At the outset I asked the self-styled Catering Wizard of the North if he thought there was anything that might be done to improve the standards of our hotels and restaurants.

'Absolutely nothing. We have not only the finest raw materials in the world but we know how to cook them to perfection. Where else would you get a nice bit of Canterbury lamb falling off the bone with goodness? All this raw foreign food makes me sick. If a thing is worth doing its worth being well done. You've got your well-done meat, your well-done greens, no skimping on the cooking. Everything well and perfectly done. That's the way we like it, and if all these foreign visitors brought up on scrag end of pit pony tarted up with foreign sauces don't like it, then they can do the other thing!'

'There are people who suggest. . .'

'I know all about that. These people ought to be shot, and I for one wouldn't be surprised if it wasn't part of an international conspiracy to undermine the whole fabric of Christian society.'

'But sometimes the quality of the food leaves. . .'

'Where else can you get a good high tea like ours with various *sur toast* specialities? Where else can you get a superb snack at any time of the night up to eight o'clock?'

'But most food writers. . .'

'I'm sick and tired of these so-called food writers whining and griping. Let them try and cook a tasty Shepherd's with all the trimmings from 9 in the morning till 5.30 at night and then see who'd complain!'

'But. . .'

'No, let me get a word in for a change! You can get a better meal here in Noshleigh than anywhere else in the world. Paris? Frogs legs and fancy knickers. Italy? Spaghetti without the toast. Don't talk to me about the Continent, I've seen it all, sir!'

'A lot of visitors find the service in our hotels. . .'

'. . .quick and efficient! None of this foreign cringing and fawning; we're above that sort of thing. We don't want these long mealtimes with people lolling over their dinner plates at two in the afternoon. In and out quickly and then they can get off to the Tower or feed the pigeons or whatever they come here to do.'

'But the food itself. . .'

'Finest in the world! But what happens when you

get to Calais? Have you ever had a good pie and chips in France, and a good unmucked-about cut off the joint with two veg? Of course you haven't and you never will!'

And our time was up.

The following week I wrote a piece for the 31 December issue of *Catering Times* promising, as a critic of the catering scene, to be more tolerant in the New Year. I listed all the things I would learn to live with: cracked cups, bad service, bland processed food, pretentious menus. Gunge leapt to the attack. A letter sped from his restaurant in Noshleigh to the Editor.

'Dear Sir,' it ran, 'I must write to protest at the so-called article by Derrick Cooper you published last week. Mr Cooper is well-known as a trouble-maker and wouldn't even know how to run a whelk stall himself, let alone telling us how to put our house in order.

'None of what he says is true. Cracked cups! What's wrong with cracked cups? We were lucky to get cups at all in the war. Stop this carping, I say. You sir, as Editor, are only kowtowing by allowing this kind of ill-informed rubbish to appear in your columns. What we want is a little more trumpet-blowing. Britain was always great and is still great to the Silent Majority. So stand up and be counted Mr Editor. Cancel this moaner's contract and let's have some cheery articles in the New Year. Good luck and God Bless.'

It was not an auspicious start to our relationship, but I was to find a much warmer side to Gunge as the months passed.

2

THE ANCIENT GUILD OF SANDWICHMAKERS

It was not until the following February that Gunge once more crossed my path. I had reviewed the new edition of the *Good Food Guide* in the prestigious pages of *Catering Times* and had drawn attention to the relative absence of good restaurants in the North. Gunge immediately drafted a letter to the Editor.

'Sir,' it ran, 'may I add small comment to the storm in a tea mug brewed up by the so-called *Good Food Guide*? The North is not a gastronomic desert. Some of the finest cafés and snackbars in Europe are to be found here. I might mention in passing the Floral Hall at Gorm-on-Sea, the Jolly Roger at Bagthorpe, the Friar Tuck Inn at Spume and any other places you care to name.'

I was later to find out that the three establishments Gunge mentioned were owned either by himself or close relatives.

'I would say to the *Good Food Guide*, the A.A., the R.A.C., and Egon Roneo,' Gunge continued, 'your activities do more harm than good! We don't need your laurel wreaths, your rosettes, your stars or your crossed spoon and forks – you know where you can put them. I am proud to say that no establishment with which I have ever been associated has ever been in any Guide and I aim to keep it that way. The people who buy and use these guides have only one object and that is to find fault.

'I think it is about time the North hit back at these moaners and groaners in the South. Who invented the fish and chip shop? Who perfected the faggot? We did. Who dresses the best tripe and polishes the proudest black puddings? We do. You will find more flambé cooking in the North than anywhere else in Britain and generous helpings of everything else to boot.

'Why do tourists flock to towns like Sunderland, Bolton and Runcorn? To look at the views? No, of course not! They come because the North is a gourmet's paradise, a fact that is well known to everyone except the knockers who run the guides. Ray Gunge. Prop.: Café Royal, Noshleigh.'

A few days later an invitation arrived to attend the ceremonial High Tea which would mark the reopening of the Ancient Guild of Sandwichmakers' Hall in Eastcheap. A press release accompanying the elaborately embossed card described how the Gothic premises, badly bombed during the Blitz, had been restored through the generosity of the Packet Soup Authority and the untiring personal efforts of the Emeritus Grand Master of the Guild, Ray Gunge, B.E.M.

Unable to get to the official opening, I made arrangements to visit the new Hall earlier in the week. A voice on the phone said that Mr Gunge himself would be pleased to take me round. When I arrived in Pudding Alley just off Scrivener's Lane a driver was unloading trays of food from a van labelled Quicksnax Corporation.

As I pushed open the chromium-plated doors of the new building a pungent blast of fried onions bellied out. It emanated not from the kitchens but from an aerosol can held aloft by an imposing figure in a white apron and chef's toque. Directing a glaucous spray over the new fixtures and fittings, he waved a cheery greeting.

'Mr Cooper? Be with you in a jiffy. I'm trying to get a nice lived-in smell, it's all too new here for comfort.' Gunge, for it was he, handed me a tin of Sprayaroma. 'That's a boiled-beef-and-carrot can I think, let's have some of that up the stairway there.' Soon the odour of synthetic beef was mingling with the onion-reek and the dense clouds of Erinmore belching from Gunge's briar.

'Funny,' said Gunge looking me up and down. 'I didn't think you'd be such a little chap; anyway you're very welcome as long as you haven't come here to run us down. I wouldn't want you getting it all wrong.' Gunge inhaled deeply and approvingly. 'There, that's better. I'll turn on the heating, get the windows steamed up and it'll be just like home.

'You don't mind coming in the kitchen do you, I've got one or two things to finish off.' He led the way to the back of the building, opened a folding

chair for me, put his pipe down, and moving to a table began spreading margarine parsimoniously on a great mountain of sliced bread.

'We've got a committee meeting later today to dot the T's for tomorrow. Now what can I tell you? First of all I think I should pay a little tribute to the generosity of manufacturers and suppliers. Renta-bloom are doing the floral arrangements in perpetuity. Messrs Hum-a-Tune have installed their Muzitape in all public rooms and Thawcook, the foilmeal specialists, are going to cater at a nominal price for our formal *haute cuisine* livery functions.'

Gunge told me that in keeping with the Guild's ongoing image the accent is on the disposable; even the Beadle's gavel is a throwaway. The waxed paper plates, the simple polypropylene cutlery sets, the mini-tubes of mustard are functional and time-saving.

'In theory,' said Gunge proudly, 'our food here will be so packaged that it could be eaten standing up with one hand in a quite restricted area. Hygienic, portable, consumable anywhere and one in-flight flexi-tray is exactly like another.'

Perfection, Gunge admitted, was not always easy to attain. 'Not all our members can afford such a high quality product in their own snacketerias, but we're rather like the Council of Industrial Design – a national show place.'

Gunge showed me the Grand Hall where there will be permanent exhibits from giant consortia like Vendakrisp, Munch-n-Crunch Ltd, Megafoods, Fropud Inc. and Scrumpijell Products. He was particularly proud of the up-to-date toilets and the gadget-packed lecture rooms where apprentices will be given advanced instruction in sandwich assembly and the preparation of a large variety of snacks from a simple cheese roll to an elaborate Cordon Bleu burger on toast *garni*.

The Guild, I gathered, represents many aspects of Britain's £450 million snack industry and as Gunge happily put it: 'We're snack-oriented as a country and hopefully it's getting better, or worse, depending how you look at it.' Gunge developed the theory that people are now eating more between meals than *at* meals. 'They can't stop – ice-creams, buns, sweets, cakes, crisps, pies, toasties, pizzas, pasties, rolls – that's the market to be in these days!'

The Sandwichmakers plan to hold open house once a month to publicise new products of which an estimated twenty-five come on the market every week. 'We're becoming a nation of nibblers,' said Gunge enthusiastically as he led me down to the members' own private snackroom. As we relaxed over a round of sardine sandwiches and paper cups of vended chocolate, Gunge outlined his personal approach to what he called 'snackology': 'The fourth Earl of Sandwich had the right idea you know, the English can't be bothered with food; what they want is something they can eat that doesn't interfere with what they're doing. I mean you can have a hot dog in one hand and still mark a bingo card with the other can't you?'

I asked him what he thought was the most seminal snack development of the past few years.

The great man pondered. 'Well, apart from the invention of the extruded continuous hard-boiled egg which I'd say was as important as the safety pin or the pipe-cleaner . . . well, what leaps to mind? Your flavoured crisps I think. If you can persuade people to eat baked-bean flavoured crisps then you're home and dry aren't you?'

Gunge tamped his pipe and struck a match. 'The next step is the marketing of a basic Ur-snack – a neutral mouthful of textured protein with plenty of added glucose to give it what we call "go-away". Doesn't matter what it's made of, soya will do perfectly well or bonemeal. With it you provide a kit to spray on the desired flavour – fishy, meaty, savoury, fruity.'

Gunge swallowed the rest of his choc-drink. 'I must get our worshipful Beadle to look at that vending machine, this tastes exactly like coffee-flavoured tea. Still we mustn't look a gift horse in the mouth.' Escorting me to the door Gunge told me what a great pleasure it had been to see the new building finished at last. 'It's a sort of temple to the Sandwich,' he said, shaking my hand, 'and I'll tell you something for nothing – there's more beauty in the simple symmetry of a well cut cheese and tomato sandwich than all your Grecian urns! No product of the potter's wheel, no sonata, no well-tuned ode has the satisfying succulence of a delicate cucumber and cress. And you can quote me!'

THE ROAD
TO NOSHLEIGH

Having met Gunge I became more curious about his background. Eventually I wrote saying that I was going to be near Noshleigh the following week and proposed a visit to his restaurant. Back came a card which said, 'Come any time you like. We never close. Ray Gunge, B.E.M.'

The Café Royal occupies a prominent corner site in Noshleigh's premier shopping thoroughfare and when I arrived outside on the following Wednesday afternoon I must confess to a tingle of anticipation. Peering through the multi-coloured Venlux blinds I could see the maestro himself sitting between the cash register and the urn cutting paper napkins in half – no task too humble even for one so eminent in his profession.

Although it was late, nearly two in the afternoon, and a large handwritten card on the door said CLOSED, I strode confidently in. Knocking out his pipe in a saucer Gunge waved me to a chair – 'No, not that one, that's got a broken leg, push the cat off the stool and sit there.' Gunge fetched two cups of strong sweet tea from the counter and thoughtfully spread a slice of Wundaloaf with best margarine: 'When you've been in the kitchen all morning you get fed up with cordon blue grub.'

One or two of the tables in the restaurant had empty Chianti flasks into which pink candles had been stuck. 'Yes, that's quite a continental touch,' said Gunge, 'we've got a cosmopolitan trade and they go for the soft lights and that.'

I asked Gunge if this was his only enterprise. 'Bless you no, we've many a poker in the fire.' For a long time he has held the catering concession at the Floral Hall, Gorm-on-Sea, thanks to the co-operation of Isambard Kingdom Gunge, former mayor of Gorm, and Ray's elder brother. The Café Royal itself (weddings a speciality, tents for hire) is no mean investment, though even the large number of enthusiastic reports sent in by Gunge's friends and relatives have so far failed to secure it an entry in the *Good Food Guide*.

The family also has a part interest in the Jolly Roger, a dine-and-dance at Bagthorpe, and the Friar Tuck Inn Motel and Service Station at Spume. Gunge, as I had established earlier, sees the North as a potential gourmet centre and tourist trap. 'And you've got to go with the times. I mean just look around; all this spells class.'

Noting the interior fittings of the Café Royal one has to admit that the Gunges have made brave efforts to create a talking point out of the décor. At that moment Thora Gunge came gracefully through the bead curtain with a tray of Melamine butter dishes which she began arranging on the tables.

'You're admiring the improvements,' she preened, 'and well you might. They've set us back a pretty penny, I can tell you. We've got lovely toilets now, Caballeros and Señoritas, and that pretty pink strip lighting over all the corner banquettes. In the receptionette or foyerette, please yourself, we've got a Benidorm theme, very sunny and away-from-it-all.'

Gunge admitted that the over-wrought iron railings round the cash desk cost £121 alone: 'Not counting the artificial grapes and etceteras.'

Thora took the cigarette out of her mouth and lunged at a fly with a rolled-up copy of the *Noshleigh Advertiser*. 'Ee, you mucky devil, they do love butter.'

I asked Gunge if he was troubled with flies. 'Not really,' he said amiably, 'you get used to them.'

Thora began laying out wicker wine cradles alongside condiments and sauce bottles while Gunge watched approvingly. 'That's a touch you don't get everywhere,' he said between puffs of Erinmore, 'elegance and style at no extra cost.' I asked him what he thought of Pamela Vandyke Price's oft-quoted dictum that wine baskets were as appropriate on a restaurant table as rolls of lavatory paper.

'Well, that's where madam is wrong! We put *everything* in the basket. Sauternes, hock, Tia Maria – I've even brought stout and Vimto to the table in a basket. You can make a good entrance and fine flourish with a basket. Kebabs in the basket, that's

something we'll have to do soon. It's getting quite popular in the South they say.'

Although the cooking is still done largely by Thora's sister Cissie, the choice is far more excitingly extended, Gunge said, than in the past. A whole new range of boil-in-the-bag classical French dishes has been added to *Le Menu*, and thanks to a technological breakthrough in the packet soup industry there are now no less than 28 *potages du jour* listed. The traditional roast for which the Café Royal has long been famous still forms the keystone of the daily lunch. As I talked to Gunge I could smell the delicious aroma of a piece of topside that Cissie was roasting thoroughly for the morrow. 'We don't put it in the slicing machine until the evening when it's cooled, that way it cuts thinner and you retain the delicate flavour. It's only a matter of minutes then to reheat your individual plated portions and add an individual Yorkshire.'

Gunge told me the family were very much involved with the Take Away craze which was sweeping the high streets of Britain. 'I think people want to identify,' said Gunge talking, as he put it, very much off the point of his head. 'It's the old hunting instinct, they want to go out and seek their food, nicely packaged no doubt, but primaeval.'

He must have seen a look of non-comprehension pass fleetingly across my features because he changed the subject. 'Lunch est servir,' he said as Thora came through with a tray of food. Over a simple meal of brawn (*terrine maison* on the menu), lettuce, slice of tomato, and Heinz Salad Cream,

Gunge told me how Take Away was changing the gastronomic face of the North.

'Look at old Charlie Budge up the road,' he said pouring generous portions of Lushwip Topping over our greengage jelly and Tahiti fruit salad. 'Last December Charlie got in on the act and now his fish shop is called the Cap'n Cod Sea Spray Fastfishery. Instead of wrapping the fish and chips in old newspapers, it goes into fancy boxes with a paper napkin, a twist of salt and a disposable sachet of vinegar. Charlie's decked himself out in seaboots, a sou'wester and oilskin and he's *doubled* the turnover. Of course he's *trebled* the prices but then that's showbiz isn't it?'

It wasn't much of a surprise when after lunch Gunge suggested we go and look at his own answer to the challenge of Take Away. As we strolled along the High Street the maestro pointed out the changes that had taken place in a matter of weeks. Trimble's Hardware had been revamped into the Pizza 'n' Paella and Miss Mooney's wool shop and fancy goods had been turned over to a Heat-n-Eat concession specialising in sausage rolls ('They're finger-pickin' good, goldarn it!')

Nearby was the Dallas-based Uncle Tom Cornpone and Hominy Grits franchise and the Brontë Black Pudding Bar-B-Q. Several launderettes had been converted to food. In fact at the Zippee Launderama some customers were still arriving at the front door with washing while others were leaving a side exit with boxes of chicken leg and french fries.

Then with perhaps justifiable pride Gunge took my arm and pointed over the road to where 'Fazackerley – Funeral Directors – Monumental Masons – Private Rest Rooms' once had its sombre office. Blazoned across the building in Mickey Mouse lettering was the rainbow legend: Butch Cassidy Cowheel Pie and Sarsaparilla Saloon. A plywood cutout of Gunge in a stetson wearing a bootlace tie and wielding a six-shooter stood at the entrance lashed down with a piece of rope to resist the Arctic winds.

'I was going to call myself Colonel Gunge but Mrs Gunge felt that was a bit, well, vulgar. I think you must keep your dignity even in catering.' Gunge told me he plans to plaster the coast from Gorm to Spume Point with Butch Cassidy concessions. 'We're getting deckchair attendants to run them, really trained people not layabouts.'

The veteran caterer waved me goodbye and as I walked down to the station I observed two workmen putting the finishing touches to the Farmer Cobleigh Black Pudding Bar. As Gunge himself had said, Noshleigh isn't called the Slough of the North for nothing.

A FISHFINGER
TO SWEEP
THE BOARD

It was in London that I saw Gunge for the third time. By now we were on first-name terms. 'Dear Derrick,' he had written with that attention to detail which I was coming to associate with the maestro, 'do come to a little shindig at Snackwrights Hall – an important announcement about food which may interest you for one of your *Guardian* pieces. Informal 6 p.m. Thursday. Do try to wear a tie. Cheers. Ray Gunge, B.E.M.'

I had just finished reading his eclectic autobiography *Frying High* and was aware of his highly respected position in the academic world of catering. His classic manual *Short Cuts in Cooking* was still required reading in most colleges and as visiting lecturer in Snackcraft at Noshleigh Hotel School and consultant to the Sandwich Board of Control he commanded deep respect in the catering common rooms of Britain.

When I joined the small but distinguished party at Snackwrights Hall I was surprised to note the burly presence of Sir Toby Gladbladder, pushing young chairman of United Bananas, the multinational consortium whose interests range from fishcakes and uranium to iced lollies and carbon fibre nodes.

It was Gladbladder who made the short speech of welcome and the announcement that United Bananas had joined with other organisations noted for their profound concern with the good things of life – the Packet Soup Authority for one – to underwrite a Research Readership in what sounded to me like fun food.

'*Fun* food?' I queried.

'No, no,' whispered Gunge, '*Un*food dear boy!'

'We are looking for a revolutionary breakthrough,' said Sir Toby, struggling to enunciate his strangled vowels clearly and precisely for all to hear, 'what we want is something comparable to the discovery of the wheel or breakfast foods or jelly. And therefore it gives us truly real pleasure to approve the appointment of Mr Raymond Gunge as our first research fellow. All the resources of our worldwide laboratories will be displaced at his disposal. This is a major development which will be of inestimable value to the Third World and in attempting to find a synthetic food which has a nutritional value consisting of lack of nutritional value we are hopefully pushing technology forward beyond the point of no return in the hope of getting really super returns for all our time and money.'

This gnomic utterance was greeted with enthusiastic applause from Sir Toby's party. More champagne appeared and Gunge introduced me to his benefactor.

Accepting a fifth glass of Bollinger, Sir Toby told me that the new food would really have to be all-purpose: 'I mean bland enough to meet all marketing parameters. It's got to sell to your Chinaman, your tram driver, your Filipino houseboy – chaps from all walks of life. We want a really viable profitmaking unfood in a sort of fishfinger that will sweep the board,' and Gladbladder sent a tray of glasses flying in his enthusiasm.

When the esurient young tycoon had disappeared with his executive minions Gunge tamped some baccy in his briar and gave me a wink: 'This could turn out to be a nice little number for me. I'm not much of a reader but we'll put the old grey matter to work and see what comes up. I think they want a sort of chip made out of waste matter . . . that shouldn't be difficult.'

Unfortunately the following week the *Financial Times* revealed that an internecine struggle for power had been taking place in the world of food manufacturing. Central Ales were mounting a massive takeover for United Bananas but while they were doing so the Quicksnax Corporation outbid them. Confusingly Quicksnax were then outbid by three other brewing barons, a situation which had been brought to the attention of the Monopolies Commission by a group of Labour MPs who felt that some aspects of the manoeuvring infringed even the mild rules of the Monopolies and Mergers Act of 1965.

I rang Gunge to commiserate and found him unusually dejected. Quite rightly he was hoping for some compensation but it seemed as if the £6,000 a year Readership was doomed. He explained that he had gone to considerable expense since the party in buying such items as a secondhand D. Litt. gown and a collapsible mortarboard in which to undertake the research.

'Anyway,' he said, rallying a little, 'have you seen any reports of my speeches about this Welsh business? I've got quite a bit of publicity up here. You know the story don't you?' I did indeed.

The chairman of the Llandudno Hotels and Restaurants Association, Councillor Jim T. Williams, had suggested that hoteliers should withdraw their advertisements from national newspapers which 'slammed' British caterers.

What gave the R.A.C. the right to describe Wales as a 'gastronomic desert'? Mr Williams asked. Especially when, in his opinion, 'the food in Wales will compare favourably with any in Britain and is certainly far superior to that of many hotels and restaurants abroad.'

This rallying call from the Welsh heartland had immediately been taken up by Gunge in his role as chairman of the British Caterers Council. In his trenchant column in the *Seaside Times & Snack Bar Gazette*, written under the sobriquet of 'Mustard & Cress', he launched a withering attack on what he called 'the *Good Food Guide* saboteurs, the fifth columnists who are bent on crippling our £6,000 million dollar-earning hotel industry.'

Gunge went on to read me a further extract. 'Are you still there? Now let's see. "I would run these mockers and moaners",' he quoted, ' "out of the country. Let them stand up and be counted by the Silent Majority. Cuisinewise the Dordogne has nothing that Dolgellau hasn't got; you can eat as well in Bryn Gawr as you can in Burgundy or Bordeaux. These are known facts only challenged by a small band of troublemakers. Wales is not the only part of this wonderful country which has been treated shabbily by the self-appointed food critics, many of whom could not boil shaving water themselves.

' "Stop it I say! Let's pull together for once. So maybe you can't get snails in Salford or fancy frogs legs in Fishguard. I would say THANK GOD YOU CAN'T! People don't want substandard offal of this kind when they can have a decent three-course lunch in pleasant surroundings." '

Gunge, warming to the cause, told me that he was hoping to enlist the help of the Festival of Light and Mrs Whitehouse herself in an attempt to staunch the flow of what he called 'the pornography of malicious and grossly indecent complaints'.

'In fact, Derrick,' he said confidentially, 'I'm going to go further. I shall go out on a branch at the next meeting of the Guild. I'm going to suggest – are you listening – I'm going to suggest that the Home Secretary should appoint an arbitrator or Omfoodsman to restrict public criticism of the catering trade. I think he should have stringent powers to insist on fair play for our beleaguered industry; the sooner unfair criticism is officially stifled the better. Then we can really get cracking efficiently. I've got to go now, there's someone at the door. Take care and God bless!'

DINING OUT
WITH A GOURMET

Although Gunge has gone on public record many times protesting that he would pay not to be in any of the guides to good eating, I often feel that he privately regrets that the Café Royal has never been included in the *Good Food Guide* or Michelin. A long letter I received from him the other day pointed out that it wasn't for want of trying: 'When they were all doing kipper pâté we did kipper pâté, when they were all doing figs in Pernod we did figs in Pernod. We've done the lot, everything from carrot and orange soup to whitebait *en croute*. We even put a special Mother Gunge's Posset on when posset was all the go but they just don't want to know.'

Perhaps that's one of the reasons why Gunge has launched his latest enterprise, a *Guide to Pubs in England* sponsored by Central Ales, the big brewing leviathan which controls 5,731 licensed houses in various parts of the country. To collect all the detail needed Captain Billy Fanshawe (the Free Drink Spotter) will lead a hand-picked team of inspectors, many of whom have spent a great deal of time behind bars. The guide is to be exclusive. 'At the outside,' Gunge told me off the record, 'there won't be more than a fraction of pubs awarded our accolade; certainly not more than 5,731 anyway.'

I asked him if Central Ales's sponsorship of the guide would in any way inhibit Captain Fanshawe's final selection. 'That's a terrible slur on a brave man with a fine record. If there are any free houses worthy of consideration for being included then consideration will duly be given without hook or crook, but I would imagine if they were any good they would have already been snapped up by Central Ales.'

Captain Fanshawe is taking the job very seriously and had already been at work for most of the day when I ran him to earth in the Whoreson Groom in a Kensington mews. He was lying in a comfortable position on the saloon bar floor and, although not able to comment at any great length, did manage to wave an arm.

Gunge has devised a unique grading system whereby every pub will be given points out of a possible thousand and there will be free holidays in Tossa del Mar for Central Ales's tenants and managers scoring over 995 points.

'We'll give', said the maestro consulting his papers, 'a hundred marks for toilets, for instance, and a bit more for those with extras like a washbasin. A hundred for doing food, you know, peanuts, pork scratchings and sausages on sticks. There'll be marks for juke-box, space invaders, one-armed bandits, bar billiards and other traditional entertainments and 500 bonus marks for the best display of Central Ales own-brand drinks.

'It's going to keep a lot of folks on their toes, especially those landlords whose turnover is a disgrace.'

I asked Gunge if this would in any way inhibit his weekly 'Dining Out with a Gourmet' column in the give-away *Noshleigh Advertiser*, a feature much appreciated by local gastronomes and the advertising manager of the weekly in question. 'No,' the maestro assured me, 'Thora and I will carry on eating out in the interests of the public for as long as we're able.'

Their jaunts have had a very useful spin-off in the last few months with the emergence of what the maestro calls his Gunge File. He outlined the scheme in a letter written in his familiar wobbly but perfectly joined-up writing:

Dear Derrick,
Herewith Number One of my new and confidental For Your Eyes Only Gunge File. As you will perceive it is a trenchant no-holds-barred analysis of selected restaurants in the North and Thora and I hope to venture further afield if the idea is well received.

The subscription is a nominal £25 a year and for that you will get up-to-the-hour reports on tip-top eateries and 2½% off the bill plus an aperitif of your choice and V.I.P. treatment on presentation of your beautifully embossed Gunge Card, a complimentary copy of which is enclosed.

With the card, across which had been stamped the word INVALID – a reference more to its uselessness than my physical condition – was a series of critiques of local restaurants.

To give you some idea of the flair for observation and the objectivity of the reports I have secured Gunge's permission to reproduce half a dozen of them.

☞ **Three Musketeers Licensed Restaurant**
Mine host 'Tubby' Tucker stood hospitably at the door of one of the region's most distinguished good food emporiums as Mrs Gunge and your columnist swept up in the hired conveyance which Tubby had thoughtfully despatched to collect us. The night was warm, if wet, and our coats were taken by a pretty little slip of a local bunny waitress in riding boots and black cape.

A bottle of Asti Spumante stood frosting in a silver cooler in the Aramis Room and while we imbibed draughts of this heady sparkling beverage and helped ourselves to mounds of salted peanuts and Twiglets, Mr Tucker in his role of patron (I use the word in its Gallic context) outlined the rationale behind his Temple of Gastronomy.

'It's really a unique combination of first-class cuisine,' he said, 'in beautiful surroundings which justifies our claim that discriminating gourmands can enjoy excellent food in a gracious setting at moderate prices.'

Tubby has been lucky to secure as *maître chef des cuisines* the former head barman from the Jolly

Spittoon in Noshleigh, who learned his culinary art
in the kitchens of long-distance steam trains on what
was the old L.N.E.R. Chef Hoggett (Pierre to the
patrons of the Musketeers) rings the changes on an
international spectrum of food, Italian, French,
Russian, Albanian and Swiss ('Knorr or less,' he
quips). All is grist to his gastronomic mill.

As we proceeded into the splendid D'Artagnan
dining-room, a cassette machine discoursed
atmospheric music and Mrs Gunge commented
favourably on the swords and halberds which had
been collected to lend verisimilitude to the Dumas
theme. Our cream of chicken soup was one of the
best we have consumed in this current eating out
series. Mrs Gunge's enthusiastic 'you can almost
taste the chicken' pleased Tubby who personally
attended to our minutest wants throughout the
repast.

The refectory table at which we sat replete with
grissini, pepper mill, and gaily decorated paper
napkins was just the right size for two. A delicious
continental dish, *coq au vin*, was then briefly flamed
by *patron* Tucker before being adorned with a
liberal helping of floury boiled *pommes* and *petis
pois au beurre*. This Lucullan centrepiece was
washed down with a robust golden Sauternes which
ideally complemented the food and enhanced the
digestive process.

To follow came jumbo portions of trifle doused
with real cream and equally real sherry and as we
sat in the lounge toying over our coffee and
respective Cocoribe and Drambuie I complimented

Tubby on the splendid collation.

Plus points: brisk and efficient service, a warm room, personal attention. Verdict. 5 stars in the Gunge File. We single out for particular praise the loos – the Knight's Room was as superbly appointed as any I have seen and Mrs Gunge later confirmed that the same was definitely the case on the distaff side. Had we paid for this meal it would have come to only £23.75 which I think you will agree is remarkable value for a first class evening out in charming surroundings as the guest of a wonderful host.

☞ **La San Remo Ristorante Italiano**

In the capable hands of Toni Flapatelli and his delightful Noshleigh-born wife this elegant trattoria is a favourite Saturday-night rendezvous for the gastronomic cognoscenti.

Toni served Mrs Gunge and myself with a pre-prandial concoction of his own creation called a Negrotoni – a cross between a Negroni and a Tizer and Tonic – while a three-piece orchestra played muted music just out of sight.

Thence we were escorted to a comfy dining-room decorated with peasant furniture mindful of the province of Soho from whence the proprietor hails. We were served with the biggest *antipasto* we had ever seen which comprised pâté, soused herring, egg slice, gherkin, coleslaw, olives, cherries, sardine, pilchard, cornflakes, tuna fish, baked beans, pearl onions, smoked cod's head, spaghetti, pineapple rings, brussels sprouts,

beetroot, croutons, Pan Yan pickle, peanuts, potato salad, Kesp balls and many another *morceaux froid* served as a little artistic gem with attendant lettuce leaves, the whole lavishly adorned with a reputable brand of salad cream.

To follow, Madam and I sampled Signor Toni's *lasagne* with fresh vegetables *au choix* including I was glad to see a very *Italiano* dish of macaroni cooked *al denture* so that it didn't stick to the roof of one's mouth or in Mrs Gunge's case her upper set. Too often in this country we enjoy macaroni only as a pudding, not realising that in its homeland it is a useful mopper-up of gravy and filling into the bargain.

Then we were treated to a flourishing display of lampwork as head waiter Pedro Rajagopalachari, a swarthy son of the southern soil, flamed some deliciously chewy pancakes in Grand Marnier and *crème de menthe*. The heat as these caught fire brought a pretty blush to Mrs Gunge's cheeks which were further enflamed by a tulip of Advocaat (on the casa) which accompanied our Cona coffee.

It was nearly ten thirty when we rose reluctantly from the table, collected our macs and umbrellas and bade farewell to our genial host. The San Remo is an eating out must. Undeservedly recommended.

☞ **Ye Olde Farmhouse, Willerby-on-the-Moor**
How refreshing to find real old-fashioned farmhouse fare in these days of make do and mend. Mine hosts, Ave and Pete Thurridge, a husband and wife team and former pupils of mine, have put first-class

teaching to good advantage in this quaint restaurant.

Sensibly the Thurridges have restricted their efforts to the simple cooking of high-class quality materials. Mrs Gunge's smoked trout with complimentary slice of lemon was perfection itself and my bowl of Baxter's game soup was served just as I like it, not too hot and not too cold, and with the welcome addition of a glass of first rate Old Curiosity Shop British Sherry.

Our main course again marked the Olde Farmhouse as a serious establishment. Eschewing mixed grill, haddock Duglère and other traditional fare, we settled for the dish of the day. This turned out to be scampi in a hot Mexican sauce which brought out the classic flavour of a full bottle of Bessarabian claret. It was, I noted, a 1964 vintage which those who know these uncompromising wines will agree was a year to juggle with.

For dessert we decided to sample the Barbados Delight – a half pear embedded in lemon jelly, enrobed in Wonderwhirl and sprinkled with crushed Cadbury's Dairy Flake. 'Ooo, how pretty,' sparkled Mrs Gunge, quite enchanted with this fairytale dish which Ava had culled from a back number of *Thirteen*.

A pleasurable meal was brought to a close with a Cornish coffee for me (a stoup of mead beneath the cream) and a pot of tea for Mrs Gunge who needed, as she said, pulling round. The scrupulously clean toilets, the gay napery and the soft pink lighting all contributed to establish a high level of gastronomic attainment.

☞ **The Ace of Spades**

This former Thirties roadhouse on the Gorm bypass
has just undergone a challenging and imaginative
conversion by Sproat, Lovage, Shrub and Lees, the
old established northern brewers, who have just
been taken over by Ing, Trilby, Bottle and
Trueflowers, part of the giant United Bananas
consortium which itself has recently come under the
umbrella of Central Ales.

Sir Toby Gladbladder, pushing young executive
of Central Ales, claimed at the opening ceremony to
which your humble scribe was invited that the Ace
of Spades is now the foremost development of its
kind in the western world.

'Young people', he said, 'need a multi-experience
when they go out these days. One discotheque is no
longer enough.' There are no fewer than seven
music areas in the new complex. The Down & Out,
for instance has a Gentlemen of the Road theme.
Patrons sit on old benches purchased from the
Noshleigh U.D.C. Parks Department and the disc
jockey is housed in an authentic Silver Lady Mobile
relief kitchen.

The real showpiece of the revamped Ace of
Spades is the Come Fly With Me Supersonic Bar.
'What we are doing here', Sir Toby explained, 'is
providing a package tour which ends in the
ambiance you find in some awful Spanish seaside
place where these sort of people invariably go.' The
entrance represents the interior of a charter jet.
Patrons sit strapped in seats and are exposed to a

full flight routine including take-off delays, the occasional emergency and a very bumpy landing. When the 'flight' is over passengers file out through the rear exit into a swinging Majorca-type bodega.

Other discos have Star Wars, Killer Shark, Moulin Rouge and Garden of Eden themes with the barpersons dressed respectively in metal space helmets, wet suits and flippers, can-can costumes and simulated fig leaves. The Star Wars Bar (To Boldly Drink More than Man Has Ever Drunk Before) serves a range of space cocktails including the Odyssey Starbanger (Advocaat and Limeade) and Blast-off (Coke, Southern Comfort, cider and sherry).

For those who don't want to dine and dance there is a wide range of drinking venues to suit all tastes. Reflecting the current nostalgia for the 1939-45 war is the All Clear which has been designed to resemble an A.R.P. H.Q. at the height of the Blitz. Sand buckets, stirrup pumps, stretchers and associated period pieces have been assembled and there are many curios on the walls: old ration books, utility furniture coupons, gas masks and a genuine air-raid siren which wails at closing time.

A tape recorder dispenses wartime bombing effects and the dubbed 78s of such all-time greats as Stainless Stephen, Suzette Tari, Clapham & Dwyer, Gert & Daisy, Stanelli, Lord Haw Haw and Nosmo King & Hubert. Drinks are served by attendants in Luftwaffe uniforms operating from the cockpit of a Heinkel bomber. To eat are Backs to the Wall dishes like Woolton Pie, Soyalink and Whalesteak

sausages and Dried Egg sandwiches. At the rear of
the pub the old building has been left exactly as it
was. The Gents with the broken washbasin and
cracked W.C., the carefully preserved graffitti, the
fag burns on the old Bakelite bar, the defaced darts
board, and a series of engravings of cats in top hats
urinating give an unmistakably timeless feel. The
only drawback is that the beer, although hygienic,
clear, sparkling, frothy, pasteurised and of a
computerised consistency, has surprisingly little
taste. This premier Northern fun complex is
undeservedly recommended for a really good night
out. Take the kiddies.

☞ The Spume Gap Restaurant (Exit 21)

Perhaps some might feel that a motorway café
hardly qualifies for inclusion within these exclusive
pages, but increasingly, local people are flocking to
Exit 21 to observe the passing scene, watch the
pile-ups and the frequent three-mile queues due to
the closing of four lanes for repairs.

On entry Mrs Gunge and your correspondent
were overwhelmed by the size of the undertaking.
The restaurant, which is heated by giant fan
blowers in the roof, has the bustling ambiance of an
aircraft hanger. You are required to take a tray and
armed with this you can proceed in a leisurely
fashion down the shining steel counters until you
chance upon a dish which takes your fancy.

On our first trip we emerged at the cash register
with empty trays but the second time round we
quickly got the hang of things and collected an

interesting assortment of comestibles. I had a
disposable cup of tomato soup, a cellophane-
wrapped rectangle of Barm cake and a Krunchie-
Wafer, a plate of baked beans, fried bread, bacon,
sausage and chips, a banana and a copy of *The
Nevada Kid* by Hank Duforest.

Now and again, green-aproned ladies scraped
food into bins and removed plates with a cheerful
clatter. Most people seemed to get through their
meal in three or four minutes, which facilitates
seating problems.

Altogether a stimulating experience apart from the
theft of Mrs Gunge's parasol. We were not able to
inspect the toilets as the queues were fairly lengthy.
Good food in informal surroundings. No need to
make reservations.

☞ The Station Hotel, Noshleigh

At the height of the railway boom and the
emergence of the region as a centre of heavy
industry, the Station Hotel was built regardless of
expense by the directors of the Great North Eastern
Railway to accommodate their passengers in style
and luxury. Modelled on Chartres cathedral, the
building still has much of its priceless stained glass
and the red brick flying buttresses and the pointed
Gothic windows reinforce the ecclesiastical aura of
this noble old pile.

A recent £300,000 renovation and bedroom
extension by the new owners, Sarasota Motels Inc.,
has modernised the property without robbing the
building of its Victorian charm. Plate glass automatic

doors, neon-strip lighting, bold carpeting and a dazzling American-style décor project a Now feel to the public rooms once heavy with cigar smoke.

A bold placard in the forecourt announces 'We Are Now Serving Breakfast, Lunch and Dinner' and 'Bed and Breakfast £17.50'. As we mounted the steps the big doors shot apart to release a wave of quadrophonic Soul music of an intensity which had Mrs Gunge reaching swiftly to turn down the volume of her newly-acquired hearing appliance.

We proceeded to the big Dallas lounge where the staff were Hoovering and clearing glasses left over from the night before. As it was by now well past noon I noted a disapproving look from Mrs Gunge which clearly indicated that had the management of the hotel been in her hands the place would have been spotless.

We took our seats in a corner near the bar where a trestle table was being set up to hold the buffet lunch. 'This should have been all done by now,' whispered Mrs Gunge as she watched a girl bring out soup bowls, condiments, sauce bottles and paper napkins.

I went to the bar where the Bill of Fare was displayed and ordered a Guinness for Mrs Gunge and a palate-cleansing half of Real Lager for myself. When the girl brought our drinks we were mulling over the menu. As the walk to the station had been a bitterly cold one and we still had our coats and scarves on we settled for a bowl of hot Soup of the Day.

'What has chef done today?' queried Mrs Gunge politely.

'Chef hasn't done nothing,' said the girl defensively.

'No dear,' said Mrs Gunge patiently, 'I mean of what does the soup of the day consist? I assume it has a flavour?'

The girl said she would go and see but she was plainly put out by this undemanding request.

'Saucy baggage!' said Mrs Gunge as the girl disappeared through the swing doors behind the bar. We sat for a bit watching the Hoovering and a flashing sign which said EXIT. Two youths with purple hair came in and attacked the fruit machine in the corner. They put coin after coin in while lights flashed and there was the roar of tracer bullets and shells but nothing came out and they left after giving the apparatus several hefty kicks.

When the girl came back she said it was 'sort of vegetable' and she poured us two bowls from the saucepan on the trestle table. It was luke-warm and had a floury taste. At 65p we both felt it was not up to scratch.

'What did you say the soup was dear?' asked Mrs Gunge of the girl who had retreated to her stool behind the bar.

'It's packet,' said the girl, 'all the soups are packet. So's the curry and the chili con carne.' This was disappointing as in order to test the skills of the chef to the full we had ordered both these dishes.

'Finished?' asked the girl after we had been sitting in silence for some time. When we said we had indeed finished she came over and in removing the bowl managed to spill soup over Mrs Gunge's shoes. I might say that Mrs Gunge behaved with impeccable restraint.

'Pardon *me*!' she said with just a touch of irony in her voice but the girl did not hear. Our main courses at £1.95 were accompanied by triangles of white bread and sachets of tomato sauce. Mrs Gunge's curry and my chili had the identical appearance and taste, only the colour was different. To follow we had biscuits and cheese (75p) each individually wrapped in small tubs. Mine was apple flavoured and Mrs Gunge's was onion and chive.

'I think,' said Mrs Gunge, 'I could do with a tea.'

We were quite ready to go when the girl came with two cups of tea already milked and sugared and a bill for £8.93.

'Shall I sign it?' I asked politely.

'You can do what you like as long as you pay it,' said the girl in what we both thought was a cheeky manner.

'Send for the manager please,' said Mrs Gunge, and from the icy tone of her voice I could see that she had 'had enough'. A burly man came bustling into the lounge and identified himself somewhat aggressively as the Food and Beverage manager. I explained that I was vetting his establishment for possible inclusion in a prestigious guide and it was not customary for a bill to be presented on such occasions. The manager pretended that he had never heard of me or my guide and said that if there was any attempt to leave without paying he would instantly call the police.

To save argument I duly paid the girl who was

hovering with a look of ill-concealed pleasure at our embarrassment.

I truly feel that I cannot recommend the Station Hotel on any level and only record this painful episode to demonstrate the lengths to which Mrs Gunge and myself go in search of good food. It was perhaps typical of the ethics of the new style of management which is sweeping throughout our wonderful industry that all attempts to recoup the outlay on this unsuccessful inspection have so far failed.

I rang up Gunge to congratulate him on his enterprise and he told me that he is confident it will be a runaway success. 'I think most people are fed up with Egon Roneo and the *Good Food Guide* and although the individual restaurants do make a small donation to the running expense of the Gunge File they receive a plaque attesting to the excellence of their cuisine, honorary membership of my Academy of Gastronomes, and a chance to buy at cost an autographed copy of the story of my early struggles, *Frying High*.

A MASSIVE INSULT TO
THE PALATE

Although Gunge's name is synonymous with catering he has always had a deep interest in wine and has always pushed its sale. On my very first visit to the Café Royal the maestro introduced me to a bottle of his own Eastern European burgundy. The packaging had been done by an art lecturer at Noshleigh College of Advanced Technology and the label depicted a chateau vaguely reminiscent of Chambord with the words *Mis en bouteilles dans les caves du Gunge* and in English *Fine Old Medium Red Sweet Wine. Ideal With All Food.*

Before I left Gunge insisted on my trying a glass. 'Mother and I won't join you, wine gives us tummy upset and bile.' The purply liquid, the colour of Quink, gave off a slightly pungent bouquet, ferrous even. It offered a massive insult to the palate and one could feel it descending the whole lengths of one's throat like a visitation of lanolin.

Whether it was the wine or the slice of veal and ham pie which Gunge proffered with it that set me off I couldn't say but I had violent hiccoughs all the way back to King's Cross. It could well be that the bottle was corked but it certainly left a nasty taste in the mouth. So when I received a press release some months later headed 'Gunge Père et Fils, Families Waited upon by Appointment. Shippers of Fine Wines since 1968' I was tempted to overlook it.

It turned out that Gunge, in association with Central Ales, was about to launch a low-priced all-purpose wine called Red Monk. Test marketed in selected areas of the North, it had already had a phenomenal success. Retailing at £2.50 a flagon (with treble stamps and a free champagne glass with every dozen), Red Monk was described as 'a pleasing blend of British and Continental wines – lasts the whole meal through, especially beneficial for nerves sufferers and the overtired'.

When, passing through Noshleigh, I queried these claims with Gunge himself, he laughed aside my doubts: 'What was it old Dr Johnson said, "A man who has a meal without a glass of wine is tired of life"? Take it from me, Red Monk will put you on your back or whatever you want in next to no time. It's a man's drink. Give mother one too. Made by monks!'

'Monks?' I challenged.

'Well, not monks exactly, all the monks have got their own brands, but we've got this retired Congregational minister, definitely a man of the cloth, and he adds a few medicinal herbs and gives it his blessing, by post of course, so it is what you might say an ecclesiastical drink.'

Gunge pointed to the label with some pride. Under the words 'RED MONK – the Divine Wine as brewed in monasteries of olde. Take one glass three times daily or drink a bottle with the one you love' was a drawing of a cheery tonsured monk in a brown habit raising a tankard to a fellow religionist busy treading grapes in what appeared to be an outsized font.

'We're also putting it out in litres for partygivers. Red Monk THE BIG ONE.' I said that with due respect I couldn't imagine nerves sufferers and the overtired would want to give a great deal of parties.

'Oh no you miss the point, Derrick. That's the trouble with you journalists, you always get hold of the wrong end of the organ. Red Monk is a drink for all occasions. Ideal for wedding receptions; that's where the gold foil cap comes in. Ideal for fish or stewed fruit; a real pick-me-up. We've even got a kosher version for barmitzvahs. Don't forget it's a patriotic wine too – made in Britain, for Britons.'

Later Gunge broached a flagon. It was the colour of violets, gave off a bouquet of boiled sweets, and pursed the mouth as might the sudden and unexpected entrance of a lemon.

'Interesting,' I said, not wishing to give offence.

'I think it presumes,' said Gunge, holding his long-stemmed champagne glass up to a red-shaded light. I asked if he thought the new line would catch on.

'Catch on,' he exploded, throwing back his head and giving a stage laugh. 'They'll be queuing for it! Just wait until you see our TV commercials. We've got a dolly bird dressed like a nun in tights on a swing in a monastery garden with these merry monks knocking it back. What's the jingle? "Red Monk will chase your blues away!" Catch on – it's going to sweep the country like 'flu!'

Some months later a press release reached me from the North. It was headed *The Big Royal One – A Wine For Her and Every Gracious Lady*. According to the handout the new wine, stable companion for Red Monk, had been heavily market-researched and tailored for all occasions.

Rose Marie, as it's called, is highly carbonated and presented in a wicker pulcianella with pink foil cap, wax seal and pink ribbon bow. The label depicts a busty girl in a flamingo pink gown poised in the courtyard of a Ruritanian castle. A Hussar officer wearing a pink busby is raising a slipper to his lips and bubbles float upwards to form the slogan 'Rose Marie I love you, I'm always drinking with you'.

'Now at last a rosé wine fit to take its place alongside Red Monk,' read the blurb. Gunge has always had a flair for catching the spirit of the times, and his pink wine appeared to have all the familiar hallmarks of success.

'We did very detailed surveys,' Gunge told me over the phone, 'among housewives emerging from bingo halls and freezer centres. We asked them very simply what kind of beverage would they wish to imbibe with the man of their dreams. It had to be pink, they said, with bubbles, pack a bit of punch and have a nice bottle. Well, Rose Marie is the answer.'

According to Gunge, the new wine is the ideal compromise for Don't Knows who can't make up their mind whether to order red or white. 'It's got all sorts of things going for it,' Gunge explained, 'not least is the special £1.99 conversion kit which enables you to transform the bottle into a beautifully artistic Tiffany table lamp.'

Gunge is enthusiastic too about the contents of the bottle. 'It's all imported wine of course. We're not revealing our sources, but it's the best that the sort of money we're willing to spend can buy. Mind you the bottle costs more than the wine, but what's cheap these days? If you want Quality you've got to pay for it.'

Rose Marie also comes in carboys for parties and polyurethane mini-flagons for round-the-clock drinking. Gunge thought at one stage of fortifying the wine with phosphorus (for brainworkers) and iron (for women suffering from anaemia) but these ambitious plans came to nought. He has also met with little success in his scheme to have the wine distributed by milk roundsmen 'for women with problems'.

A special silver-wrapped carton of Rose Marie was sent with loyal and heartfelt greetings to Buckingham Palace at the time of the last royal birth but so far no acknowledgment has been received. 'It would have been nice to have the old By Appointment on the label,' Gunge said wistfully, 'but She's very busy. And talking of busy, there's one little gimmick which might give you a para for your drinks page. You know Central Ales is going to start producing a first class Real Ale?'

I said I hadn't heard.

'Well there you are, you see you don't know everything, Derrick, do you? It's going to be brewed in time-honoured custom with genuine female hops and pasteurised wort deprived of CO_2. People no longer want the gassy beers,' Gunge volunteered, 'it's definitely back to Merrie Englande and the good things of life. Now we're going to do a special lunchtime Beefeater Beer Platter with pint of ale, slice of cheese, butter pat, pickled onion, radish and Hovis mini-loaf. That's going to be a winner. And, don't go, we're taking Real Ale a stage further and presenting Real Food. I think that's the Now Thing that really Now People want. We're going to specialise in good wholesome down-to-earth olde tyme favourites.'

Ray told me he planned to have a series of Eat-n'-Drink evenings featuring local beers and open sandwiches based on regional delicacies. 'An open tripe sandwich is obvious, but we've got other finger offerings – winkles in pastry barquettes, slices of miniature cold Toad, black pudding vol-au-vents, udder tart, all sorts. Anyway I've got to go, I'm just doing a final run-through of my entry for the Snackolympics. Don't miss it, it's going to be a cracker!'

A GOLD AT THE SNACKOLYMPICS

And what a cracker it turned out to be. Modest by international standards, a very private event, unattended by vulgar publicity, the biennial Snack-olympics were held within the cloistered walls of Snackwrights Hall, time-honoured venue for this culinary tourney.

As usual, eliminating heats held at 52 centres throughout Britain had reduced the qualifying competitors to a mere handful – fifteen men and women, skilled snacksters all, and all keyed to compete for the golds and silvers, the aluminiums and the stainless steels.

On the second and final day the atmosphere in the Salon de Thé was electric. Alone at the Long Table, Gunge was fighting to retain his right to the title of World Sandwich King. This year the trustees of the Sandwich Board of Control had tightened up security and most of the distinguished audience were watching the proceedings on closed-circuit television in the Old Vienna banqueting suite. Gunge himself was isolated from the judges and Sandwich Board officials, working behind a crimson rope barrier patrolled by uniformed Securicor guards. The hijacking in 1976 of a complete trolley of smoked salmon, caviar and pâté de foie canapés had taught everyone a bitter lesson.

'By Jove,' said a voice at my shoulder, 'what technique, what panache!' It was Lord Tonibelli, the well-known Emperor of Ice-cream. And indeed Gunge was in great form. His practised old hands were deftly creating the biggest multi-decker that even he had ever attempted; a culinary construction that gave a new and heroic dimension to the sadly flyblown word 'sandwich'.

The famous TV sports commentator who had been hired to compère the events was clearly impressed by Gunge.

'Look at this boy go! This is the big one!' The camera panned dramatically up the cliff faces of what the commentator called 'this incredible edible edifice'.

Gunge worked unhurriedly, occasionally glancing at the complicated blueprint on the table beside him, his only tools the knife, shredder, fork and spatula delimited by rule seven.

'He's going for gold now.' The tension was mounting. 'Look at the magic of this man. He's putting everything into it!'

And indeed Gunge was. Surrounded by bottles of ketchup, pickles, piccalilli and sauces, the old maestro's hands worked like flails: cutting corned beef, slicing gherkins, deftly scraping the sym-

metrical slices of Wundaloaf with finest margarine.

It seemed a feat of impeccable legerdemain as the sandwich rose ever upwards almost to the chandeliers; a great Corbusier high-rise of carbohydrates. Colourful. Triumphant.

'He has', the commentator told us, 'a deep respect for the bread. And the bread has a deep respect for him.'

At that very moment the cameras revealed a moment of potential disaster. Gunge was attempting to prop up one wing of the teetering sandwich with a Scotch egg and a delicate scaffolding of toothpicks – a brilliantly contrived improvisation which brought a crescendo of applause from the audience and whipped the TV man into hyperbole.

'This could have been, not his Waterloo but his Pisa; but see with what dazzling expertise he's back in the running again. Out front. A veritable giant. This is the alchemy of sheer genius. He's unbeatable now. What a day!'

Even when a balcony of stuffed olives threatened to fall from its penthouse of lettuce and sardines, Gunge's iron nerve never failed. A deft flick of the plastic spatula, and they were cemented back in place with a dollop of New Sandwich Spread. And then the applause – followed by a silence in which you could have heard a crisp drop.

Insolent was the *mot juste* that came to my mind, but that is not a word one associates with so humble a craftsman. And yet there was an inspired arrogance in the whole concept. Stimulated by the motion picture of the same name, Gunge had dubbed his creation the Towering Inferno.

'There go the flames,' cried the commentator as Gunge lathered the windows in his monster sandwich with tomato sauce. At the end he very slowly wiped his fingers, lowered his napkin to the table, adjusted his white toque fractionally and stepped back. There was an almost audible silence; the kind that overcomes a concert hall when the last note of a concerto fades away. Then with studied *esprit d'escalier*, the maestro scooped up a handful of salted peanuts and flicked them nonchalantly to the pinnacle of his extraordinary sculpture. They fell geometrically on to the pantiles of cottage cheese and the artistic shingles of Velveeta. It was a *coup de maître*.

There was of course no doubt about the marks. When the five judges eventually revealed their cards, there were four tens and Alderman Dripping had crossed out the nought on his card and pencilled in a one to give Gunge an historic *eleven*.

I buttonholed Mr Dripping after the applause had died away and asked him why he had broken the rules to give Gunge eleven out of ten. 'Let me put it like this,' he said, 'this man is too big for marks. He's an all time great in any company. He's a mega-snackster in a class of his own. No way could you give an artist like that a mere ordinary ten!'

Gunge himself was as calm as usual when I met him later in the robing room. He was packing his toque and his few simple implements into the Rexine Gladstone bag which he always carried with him. Was this the acme of his career?

He pondered and poured us both a cup of strong tea from the beautifully wrought ceremonial urn.

'Acme?' He stirred his tea contemplatively. 'I wouldn't say that. I did it because it was there. A man has to, because he has to, wouldn't you say? Bless my soul, dear boy, it was only a pile of bread.' Thus might Gustave Eiffel have dismissed his Tower as a load of old iron, or Cheops his monumental tomb as a pile of stones.

As he sipped his tea Gunge revealed that at one stage of his forward planning he had thought of making a Concorde sandwich: 'Tomorrow's speed-wich today, sort of thing. I was going to call it Snack 2 and use a lot of caviare and smoked salmon but I decided that a Towering Inferno would be more of a challenge. Anyway it's not winning but trying that counts. And I must say that some of my fellow competitors have been very trying. I mean anyone who seriously uses baked bean sandwiches as an infrastructure needs examining – like building on quicksand that is. And I personally thought the idea of green jelly jamwiches was far too permissive, but then I don't make the rules any more, do I? Let the best man win, that's my motto!'

PUTTING A
MESSAGE IN
THE POTTAGE

Every October the *Seaside Times & Snackbar Gazette* organises a junket and trade fair to which all those who are concerned with holiday catering are invited. I well recall the year when the venue was bracing Gorm-on-Sea, the aptly dubbed Nice of the Wolds, and in January bracing it certainly was. At the inaugural lunch I found myself sitting next to Gunge, there in his capacity as vice-president elect of the Pier Steering Committee.

He had just delivered a trenchant plea for more variety in seaside catering and his address ('There's Gold in Them Thar Golden Sands') had received a standing ovation from the cosmopolitan audience which included ice-cream manufacturers, candyfloss concessionaires, burger franchisees, town clerks, Punch and Judy artistes, soft drink tycoons and pizza executives.

Gunge's ingenious blueprint for unattended all-weather robot Autosnax with built-in Rentatune musical facilities turned out to be one of the most challenging concepts of the two-day seminar. But it was not of these summer matters that we talked but Ray's ambitious plans for a series of speciality Sunday evenings at his restaurant in Noshleigh.

Just as the Café Royal in Regent Street, one-time haunt of *fin-de-siècle* artists, is the glittering crown jewel in Lord Forte's catering diadem, so Gunge's own Café Royal in Noshleigh is the *pièce de resistance* of his burgeoning food empire.

'The gastronomic event is a trend', Gunge told me, 'that we in the North have been slow to exploit. If they can do it in London we can do it even better!' As he savoured the full bouquet of the Mateus Rosé which accompanied our turkey roll *chasseur*, Gunge outlined his plans for Christmas and the coming year.

'We had a trial run in the summer. It was a pastry evening featuring a wide and mouth-watering presentation of flans and suchlike. Tarts on Sunday we called it after the devotional programme Yorkshire TV used to do. We had *quiche* Noshleigh, a kind of bacon and egg tart but using offal and onions, and all sorts of savoury things and of course Bakewell tarts and various jam tarts, etc.'

Gunge told me that the dinner turned out to be rather stodgy so for the first menu of the winter season he was devising an International Evening featuring five courses from five continents.

'I'm mounting an exotic Australian dish to start with,' the maestro said, 'Kangaroo soup with Kalgoorlie Krootons. Then we move on to a fish course from Scandinavia, a tasty open pilchard smörrebröd with traditional tomato sauce. The main course is an exotic chop suey from Peking which our guests will eat with authentic giveaway chopsticks. After that we return to Olde Englande for a rich sherry-wine trifle and then a *sur toast* savoury, perhaps spaghetti on horseback. To follow – Caribbean coffee and Polo mints.'

Gunge now believes it is a fallacy that the British dislike foreign food. For the November evening he has invited Señor Hardwick of the Hotel Flamingo in Torremolinos to mount a typical Spanish dinner and the brochure which Gunge produced for me gives a tantalising foretaste: 'For the first time in Noshleigh a truly flamenco experience from Spain's deep south. A meal reminiscent of the towering Nevada mountains, the sparkling sea and the burning Andalusian sun, eaten *alfiasco*.'

The food aims to be in every respect a facsimile of the cuisine offered on the very best package holidays. 'Bill Hardwick is a Noshleigh man himself and he's been catering for tours for the last ten years. He knows what people like. I mean his paella is not the kind of stuff which gives you the Spanish trots.'

Early in the New Year Gunge hopes to invite a complete brigade from a top Calais café to do a Naughty Nineties evening, plus a can-can cabaret put on by a team of frou-frou tots from the Madame Pearce School of Mime and Tap. 'It requires thought,' said Gunge, 'and a certain amount of attention to detail, but in the end it's very worthwhile. A quality evening of this nature attracts a lot of favourable publicity and shows you're putting yourself in the international league.'

March will bring an Alpine Soirée with a Hunt the Swiss Miss competition. In April there's a South Seas Evening with various Hawaiian delicacies from paw-paw to tinned lychees, and in May a religious night features Muslim, Hindu, Jewish, Mormon and Presbyterian dishes. I asked Gunge where he saw the trend leading?

'Well the combinations are legion aren't they? There's no end to what you can't do if you've got enough get up and go. Eating is no longer just the old knife and spoon operation, it's become an experience, a Happening if you like. The Meal is the Message, as Field Marshal McLuhan said. And by the way our Xmas message is a Tiny Tim Happening.'

Gunge told me he had been re-reading *A Christmas Carol* and his ambition was to bring that very warm experience alive. 'I'm getting my little grandson Brett to dress up as Tiny Tim and we'll give him a little crutch and he can hop about with bread and things. I've booked three senior citizens from the Eventide home, and they'll be in Pickwick, Scrooge and Bob Scratchit outfits. Have a Dickens of a Christmas with Santa Gunge is our theme – and look at this for a slap-up menu.'

Gunge passed me a cracker and plum pudding-wreathed card with the legend 'God Rest Ye Merrie, *Bille of Fayre*' which read:

*

Ye Wenceslas Soupe with dash of sack
Slice of Foule with all ye trimmings,
sprouts, ye pease of ye garden with
knobbe of butter

Pouding Xmas with three star brandy
butter and ye Creme Toppynge
North Pole Coffee and Eskimo
Mint or confection of your choice

*

I said it looked very attractive. 'That's just the food, but there's lots of extras. All the waitresses will be in doublet and hose, there'll be a big Xmas tree and I shall enter, as we dim the lights, with a sack of seasonal gifts – bath salts for the ladies and Central Ales ashtrays for their escorts. Already this is a sellout and no wonder. For a nominal £19 they've got a complete meal experience plus cracker, plus half a bottle of Château Gunge or one small beer, plus a Novachord artist, a Santa event and carols in the street outside by the Methodist Mission if they're passing. I mean I must be *daft!*'

Gunge elaborated his thesis after lunch when he presided over the final session of the seminar. He propounded the case for theme cafés in these fighting words: 'We must market more than the meal on the plate to survive. Places like Gorm must become the gateway to romance and glamour. Let us put fiesta into Frinton and carnival into Clacton. Do as I'm going to do in Noshleigh, bring the world to their doorstep at very little extra charge.'

FLY BROTH, MUFFKINS AND NIDGET PIE

It was only a few weeks later that I was once again on my way to Snackwrights Hall for an exclusive interview with the world sandwich king. 'Dear Derrick,' he had written, 'I think you ought to know what we in the North are doing about this Tasty England gimmick. I expect you've heard about it?'

I had indeed. It was a praiseworthy campaign launched by the English Tourist Board designed to recreate a due and proper regard for indigenous dishes. Hotels and restaurants were to be encouraged to throw away their packet mixes and use local raw materials to produce traditional food. As my old friend Sir Alexander Glen, then Chairman of the British Tourist Authority put it: 'Time was when the British were renowned throughout Europe for their good living, for splendid native dishes and for their uninhibited enjoyment of fine food and drink.' It was hoped that 'A Taste of England' would hasten the return of those glorious days of yore.

'I shall be down in the metropolis next Thursday for a Carbonated Drinks sub-committee meeting. If you would like an off-the-record briefing be kind enough to present yourself at the usual venue at 4 p.m.,' the letter ended.

Shortly before four I turned into Pudding Alley and climbed the steps to Snackwrights Hall. Gunge received me in an upper room clad in a black jacket and spongebag trousers, an outfit which lent a funereal dignity to his person.

'Come into the sanctum sanctamonium,' he cried. 'Give us your mac.' As I had no mac this put me at a temporary disadvantage but Gunge was not fazed. 'Now what do you want to know? It's about the old Tasty England isn't it? Fire away and I'll try to help you with whatever is relevant.'

Gunge pushed across a menu headed Bill of Fayre, the edges decorated with rustic figures: ploughmen chasing milkmaids, parsons goosing serving girls, and arcadian couples disporting among hay stooks.

'I got a young chap from Noshleigh Art College to run that up for me and I think you'll agree he's done a lovely job. Now you know the philosophy behind all this, don't you? It's all to do with reviving the old pies and puds and things. Mind you we've been into this for ages as you know. Our Mother Gunge's Posset has won international awards, so it's nothing new for us. Anyway we're glad the Tourist Board has caught on at last and fallen into line. Cast your optic on the menu and tell us your thoughts.'

'Try,' read the menu, 'the real Tasty England at the Café Royal and dance to olde tyme musick provided by the Novachord Duo. Real Englishe Foode in an authentic English setting. Book Now.

Deposit essential to avoid disappointment.'

It was difficult to deduce from the names of the dishes what might eventually appear on the plate. I noted Noshleigh Fly Broth, 'prepared from an old monk's recipe', Sardine Savourie with twist of lemon, Troute Nell Gwynne, Nidget Pie and Spotted Bolster Cake.

There was a varied selection of puddings – Lumpy Flummery, Pishmish Tart, Muffkins, Frimmity-frommety-froo, Fat Nellie, Old Man's Hinny, Wigan Fig and Liquorice Crumble, Doddie Billybuns and Happit Bumcakes. None of it sounded very appetising and I said as much.

'Appetising,' Gunge trumpeted. 'This is the stuff of kings. Food from the heartlands. It's warp and woof, Derrick. Part of the fabric. . . . Bless my soul. Unappetising? Rubbish!'

I suggested that a lot of these dishes had died out because they weren't very pleasant to eat, but the old maestro would have none of it.

'You take Noshleigh Cold Pot, that's really tasty. A traditional stew served on washing day when the copper was being used for other things. A lovely melts and lights dish with swedes and mangel wurzels. And then there's a really cracking little delicacy my grandfather used to enjoy after he'd lost his teeth – Gorm Gruel. It's a cross between fermity and frumenty with bicarbonate of soda, sour milk, dripping and bacon rind.'

Gunge told me that although the Café Royal would feature meals typical of the immediate area he was also proposing to range far and wide to bring a real Taste of England to the North.

'There'll be Snapbag bread, that's made with flour, lard, treacle, rennet, oatmeal and stout. Lovely with a slice of Flopdale cheese.'

I asked the maestro what Flopdale cheese was. 'Well that's very rare these days. You need to know where to get it. There's just a few old folk making it up in the Dales. It's very hard, you have to take a saw to it. Tastes a bit like chalk. The Vikings brought it here, they say.' Gunge peered into space, his eyes misted with thoughts of more stirring times. 'Then of course there's Rullins. Never heard of Rullins?' Gunge gave a dry laugh. 'And you a food expert? Dear, oh dear. Bless my soul! You'll be saying you've never heard of Knockers next. Rullins, dear boy, are small grey dried lentils we eat on Rullin Friday. You soak them for a week and then boil them for two days. Then they're fired in a kiln, pickled in vinegar during the winter and you eat them with a blunt knife. Very historic. Folk say that when the Saxons laid siege to Noshleigh the townspeople only survived after they found a sack of Rullins buried in a midden. Very costive they are too but you get a real gut reaction from them. A wonderful residue of our heritage, I'd say.'

I was almost embarrassed to ask about Knockers but Gunge was not going to capitalise on my ignorance. 'Well, Knockers are a kind of over-sized Clanger, only you parboil them not fry them. They're a bit like pemmican and you eat them with bacon fat on the side and cold tea. Go nicely with Gullybog Pudding and custard, not that anyone

knows how to make a real Gullybog Pudding these days. Most women make it more like a Farbridge Grummit and you can't get the real ingredients for Grummit either – especially mincel leaf and borage-flour. Some people use Dream Topping but it's not the same, leastways not to my thinking it isn't.'

Gunge began to sound more and more like Dan Archer and his voice took on a wistful note as he waxed nostalgic over the dishes of olde. I asked about Clangers.

'Clangers, now that be a West Country dish, my dear. A harvest food dating back to the time of good King Arthur. A bit like Stonehenge Lardy Pie without the split peas. They do say that if a barren woman ran three times round a Wessex Clanger and hurled it with her left hand over a barn when the moon was in the first quarter after St Wilfreda's Day she'd be in the pudding club before you could say "told you so".'

Gunge tamped his pipe and smiled reflectively. 'Where was I? Ah yes, what's a Clanger made of? Well its a kind of savoury dumb cake baked in the ashes of a damson-wood fire. In Dorchester they used to believe that if you ate it walking backwards to bed your intended would appear and if you dropped one in a stubble field all your kine would contract murrain and plague. That's your Clanger all right.'

Gunge told me that he hoped I would spread the word. 'It's up to people like you to sound the trumpet. It's high time to paean English food. All this foreign stuff needs putting in perspective. Have a good day and buy British. You know it makes sense!'

A FINGER
ON THE PULSES

It was nearing Christmas when I heard from Gunge again. 'Ray Gunge in association with Friends of the Bean', the invitation ran, 'invites you to a Gala Xmas opening of his new Wholefood restaurant.' On the back of the card, the Catering Wizard of the North had scribbled: 'Derrick, do try to get along, a must for your column. We're full of beans and bursting to go. Cheers!'

Clutching my Uher, I caught the 9.37 from King's Cross. Noshleigh was enrobed as usual in the effluent steam and smoke of the United Bananas animal food processing factory where the offal from fish and flesh are converted into cans of *Pussy*, *Tib-Tib*, *Rover* and *Wagtail*. The aroma of boiling bones hung like a pall over the town but one soon got used to it; my slight feeling of ill-being had quite passed by the time I turned into Noshleigh's premier shopping thoroughfare.

Here there had been many changes. The Scampitoria had been converted, since my last visit, into a Crêpe-n-Take and the Pancake Heaven opposite the Do-Nut Diner had closed and re-opened as a boutique selling ski-ing equipment, fitted kitchens and fibreglass powerboats. BUY NOW BEFORE PRICE'S RISE! said a big holly-fringed sticker in the window.

The Winefayre Liquormart had given over their window to a British Sherry Event and next door the manager of the Tortilla 'n' Tacos Take Away, in a straw sombrero and poncho, was busy spraying the Mexican Pete fibre-foam figure in the doorway with Sno-Glo. Outside the Bierkeller entrance of the Jolly Spittoon four teenagers in saffron robes, football stockings and grubby plimsolls were distributing leaflets announcing the imminent arrival of Swami Huggins, the Transcendental Holy One. 'Harry Christmas,' they seemed to say as I passed.

And then my eye fell on Gunge's latest venture. The old Café Royal had undergone an exciting metamorphosis. Painted a rich bottle green, the fascia now read THE BEAN EXPERIENCE and the window was piled with jute sacks of lentils and legumes of various shapes and colours. In the doorway greeting guests was Gunge himself, a dignified figure in a flowing kaftan and several strings of beads.

'Glad you could make it, dear boy,' he boomed, extending a welcoming hand, 'and a truly happy Xmas!' Gunge pronounced the word as if it were some form of skin disease. 'Have a cordial glass of something. There's carrot juice, apple juice, dill water, anything that tickles your fancy.'

At that moment Alderman Dripping, Chief Barker of the Guild of Northern Store Santas, rang his symbolic Santa Bell and asked that we be upstanding for a speech of welcome from our host.

'Mr former Mayor' – this was a graceful tribute to the presence of Isambard Kingdom Gunge, Ray's brother who had held that office in Gorm for a brief period in 1941 – 'Ladies and gentlemen, pray silence for Raymond Gunge: Emeritus Grand Warden of the Ancient Guild of Sandwichmakers, author, broadcaster, wine merchant. . .'

'Bless my soul,' breathed Gunge at my shoulder, 'this is too embarrassing. People don't want a long list of my achievements, however impressive they are.'

But Dripping, resplendent in his artificial white beard and reindeer boots, was in full flow: '. . . visiting lecturer in Snackcraft at the Noshleigh Hotel School, Member of the Packet Soup Authority, medallist of the most Excellent Order of the British Empire. . .'

'For Services to Snacks,' whispered Gunge.

'. . . sometime Research Reader in Unfood at Noshleigh Hotel School, Fellow of the Dried Food Institute. . .'

'That'll do,' interrupted Gunge, rising to his feet, 'otherwise we'll be here all night. I'm not going to keep you for long, there's a delicious tuck-in as you can see.' Gunge waved expansively to three trestle tables laden with paper plates and cups and a selection of cold food awaiting consumption.

'Bean cuisine. That's the name of the game. And

let me say at once, beans are good news. Beanpower is here to stay. I was reading an article only last night in *Reveille* or some such which said that if you plant one acre of soybeans you can feed 77 humans for 13.1 years whereas if you stick a cow on it all you'll get is cholesterol, which eventuates in heart attacks and bad breath.'

Gunge warmed to his theme as he outlined his new philosophy of subsistence living. 'We're all in the food world here and you don't need me to tell you that the price of meat has escalated until it's hit the fan and we're left picking up the pieces. No way can you be cost effective using meat. We're all eco-gourmets now, whether we like it or not at the interface of plenty and want. My advice is don't moan, get your yin and yang moving. Make it macrobiotic not meat. East, West! Beans is Best!'

A ripple of applause broke out. As always Gunge was putting forward a bold foot to the future. 'Organic farming', said Gunge, 'is the Only Way. Bags of manure. Lots of veg., salads, raw cabbage. Good cheap soya and beans. And this time next year we'll be laughing.'

Gunge began handing out badges which said 'Make Tofu Not War' and a queue formed at the food tables. Piling a plate with roughage and indigestible-looking marrowfat peas, I moved over towards a corner where Gunge was being taped for BBC Radio Noshleigh. 'Zen? No, I haven't tasted that but we've got everything else: bean sprouts, Armenian lentils, Azuki beans, mung beans, sesame meal – all that sort of stuff. . . .'

The more I ate from my plate the more there seemed to be. Gunge, having given the name and address of the restaurant several times during the course of his interview, came across to see if I needed any of what he called 'info'. 'You just fire questions at me, Derrick. We're here to help in any way we can.'

'Well I haven't tried any myself. Had a bit of a gippy tummy lately. You don't fancy this sort of thing at the best of times do you? But I'll tell you something for nothing. This is the biggest news since fish fingers. If you're not into beans by the New Year you'll be left behind. You've got to have your finger on the pulses!'

I reminded Gunge that he had always been a great advocate of fast food. How did the bean scene fit in there?

'Bless you, Derrick, we've got a £3.50 Beanpak for the family. Butter bean open sandwich with soybean sandwich spread on the side, a cold fruit soup cup, buckwheat groats, unleavened conpah beans in corn oil, sjok and grated swede. It's going to be a real winner.'

In the corner of the room a youth in a dhoti, earring and hairband was picking at an electric sitar. 'Give us another tune, son,' Gunge cried encouragingly. 'A nice lad. He's training to be a guru or something. Comes from the Meditation Centre in Station Road. You've got to hand it to these youngsters, they're all bean-oriented. Better than bashing old ladies isn't it?'

Gunge pressed a sachet of hummous into my hand

and a bundle of anti-vivisection pamphlets. 'If you
are going to give us a bit of a write-up do mention
our all-in sitdown High Tea for senior citizens –
baked beans, chips on the side, pot of tea 95 pence.
It's a real freak-out!'

CHAPTER
11

A HEALTHY
XMAS
AND A COLONIC
NEW YEAR

In the early 1980s I was saddened to read in *Caterer & Hotelkeeper* that Ray had been admitted to Noshleigh General for observation. There was no cause for concern, the news item said, but the inference was that the old maestro was not a well man.

I immediately rang the hospital and was put through to the ward sister.

'Mr Gunge,' she queried, 'Mr Raymond Gunge? Let me see. Well, when he came in he was Only Very Poorly.'

'Only?' I asked, puzzled by this strange bit of Northern medical jargon.

'Yes,' said sister, 'not to put too fine a point on it he was dying. Anyway he decided to live and he rallied. He was Poorly for a bit and now he's on the mend . . . calling for his pipe I'm told.'

His fortnight in hospital patently had a profound spiritual effect on Gunge. On his discharge he went to convalesce in a boarding house near the Floral

Hall at lovely Gorm-on-Sea and from there he wrote me a very moving letter:

> *When you are at Death's Door, Derrick, as indeed I was for many a day recently, it makes you think. What have you done with all the talents the good Lord put at your disposal? As you know I have not been without the occasional catering triumph but I feel I needs must do something a little more worthwhile than just feeding people. There's more to man than his stomach, I think you will agree. I have decided therefore with the help of Mrs Gunge to go forth and try and spread a little more health into this sick and troubled world of ours. Make people whole just as those wonderful nurses made me whole again during my journey through the valley of the shadow. I don't quite know what I will do but I'm thinking along medical lines. . . .*

I heard nothing for months and then in the late autumn a brightly decorated brochure landed on my desk: 'Take Nature's way to Health,' it read, 'Up the M6, turn off at Gate 26, left at the Spume By-Pass and thence by the A439 to the Ranch.'

Attached was a note in Gunge's florid scrawl: 'Dear Derrick, if you fancy a massage or acne treatment, why not pay us a visit? The Great Northern Health Ranch and Natural Spa at your service.' Enclosed was a photostat of an advertisement in *Health and Energy*. Buried among the offers of herbal tobacco, wheatgerm rissoles, miracle bunion cures and frames to take the weight of bedclothes off your ankles, was a challenge from Gunge. 'Tired, run-down, nervy?' it ran. 'Put yourself in the hands of experts. Special terms for pensioners. Approved by leading practitioners and men of medicine. Book now for our bumper Xmas Fast-In. Hurry, hurry, hurry!'

Early in December, I found myself only a few miles from Spume. Slipping into a devastated phone-box, I dialled the ranch.

'Doctor's quarters,' said a carefully genteel voice. It was Thora Gunge, her voice refined as caster sugar.

'Is that Mrs Gunge?' I asked.

'Matron here,' said Thora distantly. 'To whom did you desire to speak with?'

'It's Derek Cooper here; is Ray about?'

'I'm not sure where the Director may be. He could be in his consulting-rooms. Was there something?'

At that moment, an extension phone was lifted and I heard Gunge say, 'Hello, what's going on, who's there? If it's a firm booking, take it!' When Gunge found it was me, he insisted on my coming straight over. 'I'm just doing a little bronchoscopy, looking down someone's throat, but I'll be through when you get here. Bye.'

When I drove into the grounds of the ranch, a collection of wartime huts heavily defended by a barbed-wire perimeter, Gunge was at the door of the largest, on which was written in age-old letters, 'Guardroom. Knock and Wait.'

I'd never seen the Maestro look more impressive. The chef's toque had been exchanged for a Homburg hat, the apron for a sparkling white coat. Round his neck Gunge wore a stethoscope, a tape-measure and a monocle on a silk ribbon. Several jam-sized thermometers protruded like knitting-needles from his top pocket, and he was carrying a Dr Doolittle black medical bag. Sporting a Van Dyke beard and a squadron-leader's moustache, it was not quite clear whether he was impersonating Dr Hackenbush in *A Day at the Races* or James Robertson Justice in *Doctor in the House*. Judging by his air of benign *gravitas*, it was on the latter that he leaned most heavily.

'Come in, dear fellow, there's nothing to worry about,' he boomed, all bonhomie and bedside. 'Lie down on that couch, slip your things off or weigh yourself – or sit here if you'd prefer.' I chose the upright patient's chair placed beside an enormous desk cluttered with ethical drug literature and bottles of cough mixture.

'I must apologise for the surroundings,' he said, tamping a plug of Erinmore into his briar and thrusting a thermometer into my mouth, 'but it was all we could get on the spur of the moment. I was after Mentmore, but a group of Eastern fakirs got hold of that. Now, you'll want to know what we're up to, won't you?'

I said, 'Ah,' and nodded a vigorous 'yes'.

'Well, you know Thora and I have always been trail-blazers, so to speak. I've spent a lifetime filling people up with food; here, we put tired bodies to rights. It struck us that with the price of food going up every day, if you could run a place on lettuce leaves and a few slices of cucumber, you could maximise profits no end. So we're into health now, all lemon juice and cold baths.'

Gunge seized my thermometer, clucked with disapproval and whisked me round the ramshackle huts on a quick tour of inspection. Perhaps weakened by lack of food, few of the residents were moving; they sat in deckchairs watching black-and-white television. 'Of course, we're not in top gear yet; we're planning, hopefully, several 18-hole golf courses, helipad, swimming-pool, riding stables – a real home-from-home for overtired executives. We aim to be the finest health complex in western Europe. You'll be able to have your mud-baths, dandruff therapy, electric shocks, urinalysis, manicure, facial – anything you want.'

I asked Gunge about his medical back-up. What would happen if some old party took a turn in the steam-room?

'Well, I've got the St John Ambulance on tap – they're a wonderful bunch – and Mrs Gunge worked in her single days as a dentist's receptionist, so she's used to moving in medical circles. During the war, I was in hospital catering myself, and we both have a pretty thorough medical background. And of course I picked up quite a few tips during my little spell in hospital. As far as I can see, half these chappies in Harley Street are just plain misters like myself – it's all common sense, isn't it? And as I always say, faith will heal mountains!'

As we sat over a beaker of seaweed tea in a hut labelled 'Operating Theatre – Q here for Appointments', Gunge explained the philosophy that lay behind the ranch: 'Gluttony is out, it's all abstinence and starvation; that's your biggest growth area in catering – not catering at all! Look at the French, all living on steamed shredded carrots. Look at the Americans, scared to death of fat. "Starve a friend for Xmas," that's our motto. We've got a special gift voucher scheme you can buy in most health-food shops, which will give a couple four Yuletide days here at the ranch and guarantee they go home hungry.'

Gunge showed me some of his Christmas menus; Boxing Day was devoted mainly to cabbage water and melon seeds. I said it sounded a bit depressing, unfestive.

'Depressing? Bless my soul, not a bit of it. We've got all the non-toxic manifestations of the festive season: crackers, electric log-fires in most public rooms, paper chains, flameproof Xmas trees, but it's all built round my own version of *cuisine minceur*. Mince pies minus the carbohydrates, Christmas pud without the killer kilocalories. You'd better tell your readers to get on the phone if they want a last-minute booking; we're getting absolutely packed out.'

Gunge told me they had a Christmas Eve non-dinner dance for the Noshleigh Nephalist and Vegan Ashram, and a large party of cycling fruitarians booked in for Christmas lunch. 'That really solves the cooking and washing-up syndrome; all they need is a side plate and a fruit knife. Then we've got the old folks' beano – they're coming for a Low Tea on Boxing Day. We shall give them all a vibro-massage on the house, a cold plunge, a quick go in the sauna and then a salad and a singsong.'

'What about yourselves?' I asked.

'Well,' said Gunge, polishing his monocle, 'I've got a crate of something in the sanctum sanatorium; you mustn't lose all sense of proportion. I mean, if we starved to death, how would all these good people manage?' and, like a latter-day Schweitzer, he waved a caring hand to the barrack square, where a group of painfully-thin patients were trying to do press-ups.

'Now I'll see you out. I've got doctor's rounds at four. Keep taking the bran, and if you want a colonic irrigation in the New Year, you know where to come.'

On the threshold, I held out my hand and Gunge solicitously grabbed my pulse. 'Very dodgy, Derrick,' he diagnosed. 'A fortnight here could work wonders for you. Tone you up no end. Think about it and God bless!'

WE LIVE IN A
GLOBAL SNACKBAR

The most prestigious provincial food event of the year is undoubtedly NORCATEX, the bi-annual Northern Catering Exhibition which attracts foodsters from all over Europe and from as far as Tasmania and the People's Republic of Tashkent.

Situated in the echoing Great Northern Exposition Complex, NORCATEX is a dazzling window on the world of futurefood. In six interconnected halls some 2,500 organisations had taken stands to create, in the words of the organisers, 'a truly international show-piece for the hotel and catering industry'.

I arrived early on opening day and wandered among the dazzling range of booths presenting everything from disposable paper chef's hats to fully packaged motel bedroom units. Despite the highly efficient extractor fans, the blue haze of heavy-duty frying oil and the odour of hundreds of appetising new savoury products hung in the air.

The ground floor of the Main Hall was devoted to

the very latest gadgetry and hi-tech hardware. The eye fell on gastronorm convection steamers, laser vending machines, boilerette cookware, lava stone char broilers, buttoned vinyl bidets, hickory smoke-aroma units, purpose-built burger chutes, dedicated juice systems and step-in turbo chillers.

An enterprising sales girl dressed as a pussy cat tried to sell me a consignment of coextruded bendy straws, personalised electronic swizzle sticks and a giant arrangement of polysilk flowers. 'Turn your franchise into Kew Gardens,' a placard said.

Eschewing offers of pot pourri bath gels, Eezi-care polycotton doilies and shake-on flavour mixes, I took the escalator to the first floor where smaller firms were exhibiting the latest developments on the fast food front: do-it-yourself noodleburgers, self-inflatable canapés invented by Innerjiffee PLC, disposable polystyrene *vol-au-vents* and exciting new lines packed in nitrogen-flushed sachets with names like Wundafill, Miracle-Mix, Flavorspred and Junkee.

'Heartening, isn't it?' said a voice at my shoulder. 'I'd go so far as to say you wouldn't find a more pretentious display anywhere.'

It was no surprise in this glittering scene of marketing and mayhem to encounter Gunge, he who stands head and shoulders above other folk heroes on the food scene. Beside Gunge the boffins who perfected the tensile crumb for the fishfinger revolution, the pioneers who devised dessert toppings, instant pot snacks, and pizza dough that sticks to the roof of your mouth like lint fade into the background of anonymity.

I asked Gunge how his health spa and clinic was prospering. 'Oh, we've moved on from that, Derrick. We had such a success rate that eventually there was no one left to cure. We had a little takeover bid from a Private Care group and I think it's become a nursing home for the confused. That's a growth market if ever I saw one, but I needed more of a challenge myself. Something will turn up. Meanwhile mother and I have resumed our full-time role at the Café Royal. I need my stoves you know.'

Gunge breathed in deeply; the smell of texturised Krinklies, mock bacon strips and fried pizza-flavoured onion rings obviously enchanted him. 'Mouthwatering, isn't it,' he said, waving expansively to a salesman in a white top hat on a stand emblazoned with a banner reading 'A Bun is as Big as All Outdoors'.

'Tried our blockbusters, *cher maître?*' asked the rep, steering Gunge into his inner boutique and placing a flexi-cup of Café de la Paix *vin mousseux* in his always receptive hand. 'This is really something new in space snackery.' He reached into a deepfreeze and drew out a solid object wrapped in Klingfilm. 'There, what do you think of that?' he asked, exposing it to our gaze. It looked to me not unlike a deep-frozen elephant's stool.

'That seems to me like very good news,' said Gunge, prodding the thing with an educated finger.

'Rock hard,' said the rep, bringing it down on the table with a karate blow. 'There! Ah, so! Not even chipped. But in twelve seconds you can microwave it into a perfect steaklette oozing with simulated full cream dairy cheese. It's got fabulous come-back-for-more appeal, a full-of-good-things taste, great meal-in-itself satisfaction and Big Big Flavor. We've tenderised it with Salivin, it's charcoal-sprayed, sugar-enriched and full of salt. Free range Macropus, prestressed for long shelf-life, that's the secret.'

'Macropus?' queried Gunge.

'From Australia,' said the rep.

'Beef?'

'Kangaroo, actually,' confided the rep. 'Rich in cornflour, niacin, riboflavin, lecithin, everything you need for a fully balanced snack operation. Try some.'

We were handed portions on sticks.

'Nice and chewy,' approved Gunge. It tasted a bit like a glove. 'Very entrepreneurial,' he said, bestowing his imprimatur. 'Should do a bomb!'

Thanking the delighted snackster Gunge and I left the stand. 'If you want a story, Derrick,' he said as we processed down the aisles, 'stay close. I'm about to spring a bombshell that will stand fast food on its head. I've got a little soirée organised in the Exhibitors' Lounge at noon but I want you to have a dekko at our *Salon Culinaire* first. I think you'll be impressed.'

On our way we tried a score of heavily processed products, many of which left the tongue feeling as if it had been abraded with wire wool. They were not meant to be eaten so much as crunched and champed. When you snapped them they parted with the report of a pistol shot; the noise ricocheted round the inside of your head quadraphonically.

'Very *noisy* food,' I ventured.

'Food has to be sonorous,' said Gunge. 'We've researched all this exhaustively and a snack has negative appeal unless it is audially assertive. What people want from the eating experience is reassurance; it reinforces their persona. Snacks must crash, bang and pop. I mean you wouldn't want a snack to wheeze would you? It must say, "Here I am. Pow. Eat me." ' He made it all sound a bit adventurous – like being mugged.

'Ah! Here we are,' said Gunge, gently pushing through the crowds. 'The *Salon Culinaire*. A little bit like the Royal Academy summer show, I often think. It's the more artistic, sensitive side of catering where our budding Tretchikoffs make their mark.'

Laid on long tables were hundreds of edible still lifes, many of which, Gunge told me, had taken months to fabricate. Most of the rosettes seemed to have been won by the Royal Army Snack Corps, if only by the sheer weight of their entries.

'That's a beauty,' said Gunge, and pointed with admiration to a Chieftain tank made out of fifty loaves of bread, eight dozen hardboiled eggs, twelve pounds of chipolatas and a gallon of béchamel sauce.

'And this is your *Table d'Honneur* – reserved for work of superlative merit done by the Laureates of International Snackcraft.' Here were displayed the most intricate and tortuous works created from a variety of substances. There was a working model of Jimmy Savile with illuminated cigar sculpted entirely from lard. Princess Anne in milk chocolate was leaping a marzipan Beecher's Brook astride a

SALON CULINAIRE

mocha hunter. A pulled sugar representation of a Come Dancing final stood alongside Our Lady of Lourdes in royal icing ('very devotional,' said Gunge reverently) and the centrepiece of the room was a candyfloss tableau of Margaret Thatcher and her husband Denis waving from the doorway of their gracious Barratt mansion home in Dulwich while the Queen looked on approvingly surrounded by a pack of pastillage corgies.

'There's a lot of social comment here,' said Gunge, pointing to a potato work re-enactment of the official signing of the Channel Tunnel agreement in Canterbury cathedral. 'And of course sheer beauty.' He drew my attention to a boiled lobster set on a mirror flanked by prawns, scallops and marzipan chips with a border of roses and daffodils piped in patisserie cream.

'I'm glad you could see this,' said Gunge expansively, 'snackery isn't all titbits and crisps. We have our more intellectual side even if we don't get the coverage we deserve from the media.'

We made our way to the Exhibitors Lounge where some of the most influential figures in the industry, alerted by a sixth sense that Gunge was about to bowl a googly, had gathered to attend upon the old maestro.

Soon Gunge was holding court in his easy and charismatic fashion, surrounded by video games reps, carbonated drinks tycoons, burger executives, cookie concessionaires and assorted hucksters all waiting for the one-liners for which Gunge is renowned in the brittle world of international snackery.

In rapid succession he introduced me to a man with a monocle who travelled in eutectic soup urns, a food behaviourist from the Toffee and Chocolate Alliance, and the Founder-President of the Sauce and Condiments Council. Then Sir Toby Gladbladder, Honorary Chairman of the NORCATEX Organising Committee, tapped on a glass to command attention.

'Friends,' he said, smoothing a lapel, 'we are gathered today to hear a few well chosen words from Mr Fast Food himself.' There was a round of discreet applause.

'I refer to Raymond Gunge, as visionary a genius in the world of the 1980s as the great Carême was two centuries ago in the 1780s. Ray, it's all yours!'

'No friends,' said Gunge modestly, 'it's all yours. I am an old man, youth is on *your* side. Hopefully we will look back on this year as the watershed, the turn in the road at the end of the long hall. There are no easy cornucopias, no sense indeed in cutting corners.

'With the help of the Snack Research Association we have come up with just a few little ideas for Very Fast Food which you will all be able to taste in a moment or so. Nothing definitive, you understand, just pointers towards the future. But all the food is handleable – it is what you might call a gastronomy based on fingertip control. A normal healthy punter could eat his fill in four minutes – fifteen customer units processed per hour. Magic!'

Gunge descended from the small podium on which he had been standing and took me by the arm. 'You look puzzled, Derrick,' he said, 'but like all great ideas it's dead simple.' Gunge explained that some of the morsels actually had monosodium glutamate on the *outside* so that the taste buds were pre-primed before mastication and peristalsis commenced. 'That's a wonderful time-saver. Now, point two. Everything is bite-size.' Gunge waved with a proprietorial air to the weenie-dogs, mini-pies, frittered fish fingerlings, Bar-B-Q-Bitz, Tiny Toads and assorted food gobbets.

'No wastage, no messy preparation. Everything has great eye-appeal, long storage life, warms in a trice, and each item carries built-in profits. And of course it's a really challenging range – people won't want to sit *down* to this sort of food, so straight away you've eliminated staff and tables. Acres of floorspace cleared for profitable eventuations! And of course you can munch this kind of stuff at any hour of the day and still come back for more. It's a logical extension of TVP.'

'TVP?'

'That's right. Home in one. Textured Vegetable Protein enables you to maximise anything – turns a chicken into a turkey; a bowl of breadcrumbs into fillet steak – if you add the right flavours. So marry the concept of VFF to TVP and you've got the Ultimate Answer – an optimum number of people eating not very much incredibly quickly for relatively large sums of money.'

'But what about the meal experience?' I asked. 'You said yourself only this June the meal is the message.'

'June was June,' said Gunge with a patient smile. 'We've got a new message for next year. Remember what old Field Marshal McLuhan said? "The living-room has become a voting booth." Well, Gunge says the dining-room has become a snackbar. Just as the wheel is an extension of the foot, so the snack is an extension of the hand. We live in a global snackbar! Take care and remember – think small!'

CHAPTER

13

A STRIDENT ANTIPHONY

It was June before I met the Gunges again. Noshleigh is not a warm place, even at the height of summer. It has been observed, by Melvyn Bragg, that a painting of the Temperance Hall and the Jubilee Baths would make a Lowry look positively Mediterranean, but I brightened when I saw the familiar steamed-up windows of the Café Royal. Folkmyth hath it that even when the establishment is closed for what the Gunges like to call the *fermeture annuelle* the steam numinously remains; maybe it's the vaporous influence of the shining urn ever on the boil which Thora was attending when I arrived. Since her sister Cissie became bedridden she is entirely responsible for the light beverages in this popular restaurant and her imaginative hands can also be seen in the decor of the Friar Tuck Inn motel and the Jolly Roger Dine & Dance.

'Tea. . .?' she asked and the rest of the sentence was drowned by a mighty roar; steam belched out like the Coronation Scot leaving Euston. Very little had changed since my previous visit, but there did seem to be more chafing dishes than so small an establishment might merit. Seeing my eye fall on them Thora said, 'Have you seen father with the lamp?' She spoke with the veneration of one discussing the exploits of Aladdin.

Later I was to have the privilege of watching Maître Gunge (in his famous white sharkskin tuxedo and clip-on tartan bow tie) prepare his masterpiece *Scampini au Sauce Champagne*. The timing with which Madame Gunge hands him the Babycham and the bravura with which he sears the succulent double-glazed freezer prawns is one of the great gastronomic sights of our time. The orange and blue flames leaping up to the Perspex chandeliers present a chiaroscuro which the Arts & Crafts editor of the *Noshleigh Advertiser* described in a memorable phrase as being 'like a Turner setpiece come to life'.

'You know,' said Thora, 'that father has just been intronised as a *Chevalier* in the *Confrérie des Snacquevins*?'

It was snackdom's highest accolade and indeed one of the reasons that had brought me North. The gourmet magazine *Gluttony* had commissioned me to write a profile of the mercurial maestro. A colour piece they said. What was happening up there – in the *North*? The editor pronounced the word as if she were describing an archipelago of permafrost and terminal deprivation. Were people eating *anything* AT ALL, she seemed to be asking. It was a challenging assignment which of course I could not resist.

'Ask him about additives,' said the editor, 'real food, that sort of thing. Do they *know* about *REAL FOOD* d'you think? Is there a *cuisine nord*? I mean they must eat SOMETHING!'

So here I was and here with a flourish was Gunge coming through the door, hanging his mac up, demanding tea, radiating bonhomie.

'An article,' he said, 'of course. Fire away. What do you want to know? Something about my new award? Pass the insignia, mother, will you?'

Thora produced the elaborately engraved EPNS teaspoon suspended from a heavy chain and Gunge donned the utile regalia with some humility.

'The insignia', he said with quiet pride, 'of the *Confrérie des Snacquevins.*'

'Snackdom's highest accolade,' I said.

'The highest,' Gunge concurred with suitable *gravitas.* 'Not of course to be worn with my B.E.M. Now that of course is a *Royal* honour. From Her. But I am happy to have both.'

At the time of this meeting with Gunge the food industry appeared to be fighting a rearguard action in the face of mounting criticism from the medical profession that many of its products were positively harmful to the nation's health. Despite enormous sums of money spent by transnationals like the Quicksnax Corporation providing schools with videos and free books outlining the nutritional desirability of their various products, public opinion seemed to be turning against them.

In a massive attempt to halt the health lobby the Sugar and Salt Trust – a non-profit-making totally independent registered charity financed by the sugar and salt industry – had invested £250 million in a TV and sports sponsorship campaign designed to reaffirm that sugar and salt were naturally occurring foods free of all additives and essential elements for health and strength.

A major breakthrough had occurred in March 1986 when the Professor of Nutrition at King's College, London concluded after a twelve-month study financed by the Snack, Nut and Crisp Manufacturers' Association, that crisps contained more fibre than wholemeal bread, six times as much Vitamin 'C' as an apple, and weight-for-weight were less salty than cornflakes.

Previous reports from Professor Tomsbotham, Vendapud Reader in Nutrition at Noshleigh Poly-technic, have proved beyond reasonable doubt that toffees, slush drinks, lollies, beefburgers, Swiss rolls, packet soup, peanuts, and all heavily fried foods were also infinitely more good for you than had been previously suspected. 'One Mr Smiley Chocbar,' he told a startled meeting of the Noshleigh branch of the B.M.A., 'is equivalent to 10 pints of skimmed milk, the juice of 50 squeezed oranges, 73 lettuces, 25 wholemeal loaves and a sack of potatoes.'

Despite much helpful research of this nature the media tended to focus unhelpfully on the malign aspects of what it pejoratively described as junk food. I asked Gunge if, as a sometime Chairman of the British Caterers' Council, he ever worried about the over-use of additives and chemicals in food. He told me he was more worried about the scare-mongers and self-appointed guardians of public health who were, as he graphically put it, upsetting the apple pie.

'Look, Derrick, these additives have been rigorously tested. Many of them are a positive key and boon to health. I know people who can't get enough of them. All this talk of pesticides, hormones, and chemicals is actually *making* people ill! That's why we're about to launch DRACULA. You've heard of DRACULA?'

I said I hadn't and Gunge said I soon would. Evidently the big guns of the food and drink world had hired a public relations company to put their case to the public. The P.R. firm had set up an Additives Advisory Bureau and were about to launch a counter-blast to what they regarded as subversive groups such as FACT – the Food Additives Campaign Team and COMA.

'This kind of carry-on is enough to put anyone in a coma with sheer boredom,' said Gunge with a dry laugh, 'but DRACULA will take their mind off things.'

The word was an acronym, he told me, for Deregulation of All Additives and Chemicals Under Licensed Approval.

'It means that all the really caring, responsible multinationals will, with the approval of the government, be licensed to use any additives they like in the interests of the public. What the housewife wants is good long shelf-life and lots of colour and flavour in her food. And that's what she's going to get.'

I asked Gunge about people who were allergic to additives. 'These are known troublemakers, Derrick. They're probably very sick people to begin with and no amount of additives will cure them. Can't we talk about something a little more relevant?'

One topic which I did wish to discuss with Gunge was the new trend in smart restaurants of bedding the most unlikely ingredients together in artistic heaps on black plates. The meal as pictorial art had become a cult among the great chefs of Europe and in the pursuit of culinary painting they naturally sought out the most colourful combinations of raw materials they could find. Had not the Roualt pastiche of leeks, red crab meat, salsify, snails' eggs and bilberries created by the egregious Foie Gras brothers at their five-star restaurant in the Dordogne been hung permanently in the new Culinary Arts Centre in Paris?

In Britain scores of young restaurateurs struggling to attract the attention of the *Good Food Guide* were engaged in frenzied attempts to outvie each other. It had not been a good period for leaving well alone. I had come across an increasingly eccentric range of culinary combinations: scallops with framboise, prawns bathed in orange yoghurt, duck with honeyed lychees, kipper and capers *tiède*.

Peppercorns, pine kernels, pickled nasturtium seeds, juniper berries, passion fruit, uglis and fresh limes ruled the kitchen. It was all cumin and coriander and what wasn't fennel was fenugreek. Was Gunge, I wondered, into 'gourmet' and the painting of edible pictures on plates? After all when salads became all the rage hadn't he been the first chef to bring a box of *radicchio* north of Potters Bar?

'We've been into all that, Derrick, and out the other side. Burnet, purslane, rocket, sweet cicely – we've used sweet everything! I mean I virtually pioneered the unusual in the North. Pass those menus, mother; Derrick seems to think we're still grazing on grass here or something.'

Gunge leafed through a pile of old menus which revealed dishes of striking originality. There was winkles with gin; carp stuffed with pear; sea bass with ginger, pink peppercorn and lime sauce, and *paupiettes* of salmon macerated in Jubilaeum's akvavit in a bed of dottle leaves.

'Some of this is pure poetry,' said Gunge, 'who else has thought of the ravishing possibilities of marrying smoked tuna with kumquat essence? My gulls' eggs *à la Gunge* marinated in lime with nettle and goat's cheese and marjoram marmalade is – well, a *tour de force.*'

There wasn't anything you would find at Rungis market in Paris, in New Billingsgate or New Covent Garden, said Gunge, that was not readily available in the North.

'I have the utmost admiration for the innovative ingenuity of the Foie Gras brothers and the Roux brothers and the whole lot of them but, bless my soul, there's nothing *new* about all this. We've been doing this kind of stuff for years.'

Gunge told me that he had just returned from Noshleigh Central Market where he had been

browsing among the exotica. 'I picked up some very nice mangoes this morning and I might do something special with them, stuff them with black pudding and chitterlings, and present them in a curry sauce or perhaps nestling in a chicory and endive collation with hazelnut oil. We've had a great success here with quenelles of cow-heel in rhubarb leaves and faggots wrapped in lettuce with a kiwi-fruit garnish.'

Gunge has become a great believer in the octagonal-plated meal. He has devised an authentic toad-in-the-hole that has all the majesty of a Henry Moore, and his tripe and *navets* has been likened to an edible early work of Suzuki Harunobo. 'We do,' said Gunge, with modesty, 'a quail stuffed with mulberries and elvers that is a pretty as a gouache – on sorrel sauce it's almost too good to eat.'

Warming to his theme, Gunge told me that surprise was the name of the game. 'If they want vinegar on the chips, make it raspberry vinegar. You must have humour; without the humour of the unexpected there can be no great cooking. Nowadays a *patron* must astonish his clients. Look at Anton Mosimann down at the Dorchester. Remember his soup covered with gold leaf? Pure genius. Exactly like my famous Pontefract Chop. It was a *coup de théâtre* if ever there was one.'

I remember Gunge's Pontefract Chop very well. There was the simple statement of the double kidney cutlet, a small punctuation of green, pink, red, black and yellow peppercorns, like so much Dolly Mixture, and then the ultimate but gastronomically appropriate impertinence – a single Liquorice Allsort with its strident black and yellow antiphony, poised on a small slagheap of snow-white potato.

'I think,' said Gunge, reflectively, 'that really said it all. Mind you, some have been kind enough to say that I surpassed even that with my udder dish.'

'Which other dish?' I asked.

'No,' boomed Gunge, testily. 'Udder. Not cow's udder but calf's udder. The Foie Gras brothers wouldn't know what to do with that, would they?' And there was a Northern challenge in his voice.

Gunge, venturing on to the frontiers of *cuisine bizarre*, had marinated the udder in sarsaparilla, sliced it into goujons, then interleaved it wth alternate layers of dock and nettle, poached it in coconut milk with pickled turnip, and moulded it to make a spectacular terrine relieved with nuggets of orange and red peppers. What gave it a final and unassailable authority was the lake of puréed banana and durian on which he served it.

'I thought to myself,' said Gunge, 'that it might be a little too understated, but I think it worked. Simplicity is all, don't you agree?'

MEMORIES OF A
MORE GRACIOUS AGE

For some time there had been rumours circulating in the hotel and catering world that Gunge was about to retire; to doff his toque, lay down his knives and fold up his apron. Then a small paragraph in *Catering Times* caught my eye. Under the headline 'Gunge Goes Country' it suggested that the maestro was looking for a rural hotel on which he could impose his own special signature.

This was perhaps not unexpected for it was to the country that the *prominenti* were scurrying. It was a movement which started in the English Lakes in 1949 when Francis Coulson began serving splendid teas at Sharrow Bay. Others copied him, opening *restaurants avec chambres* in old houses set in idyllic surroundings. Soon ambitions rose. The houses became bigger and grander. Castles, manors and shooting boxes no longer supportable by the stranded gentry were converted into luxurious watering holes for Americans who came flooding into Britain waving cheap dollars and commandeering chauffered Daimlers to take them on the milk run round Oxford, Stratford, the Lake District and on to Edinburgh and the Highlands.

Strewing their path they found a succession of country seats newly converted to the sanitary world of bidets but retaining their old-world charm. Some had great gardens, others were noted for their commanding views, but all had one thing in common. They were very expensive. But then it was not only bed and breakfast you were paying for but history, heritage and the privilege of staying in stately homes 'redolent', as one brochure put it, 'of a more gracious age'.

None, it turned out, was to be more dramatically redolent of everything a country house should be than Gunge's final professional venture.

'At last,' said the brochure, 'the ultimate country house experience. Hardtack Hall is everything you always wanted but never thought you could afford. A world of bygone splendour conjured up at the flash of your Diner's Card. Spoil yourself and a loved one at special weekend prices.' I knew that this would be no ordinary country house hotel, for nothing that extraordinary man the self-styled Catering Wizard of the North did was untouched by his own special genius and his capacity for going just one step beyond everyone else. Exceeding the Norm, he had called it once, stretching oneself Beyond the Possible.

The frontispiece of the brochure featured an artist's drawing of the grounds and gardens surrounding Hardtack Hall. Rhododendrons and

azaleas were in vivid flower, a group of languid Edwardians were playing croquet on a lawn, while in the distance a row of Norfolk-jacketed toffs were bringing down pheasants like dandruff from the untroubled skies. 'Relive the memories of a more gracious era,' said the caption, 'when Britannia ruled the waves and it was always eternal June.'

Inside the brochure was a personal letter from Ray Gunge. 'Dear Derrick,' it ran in his arachnoid scrawl, 'I don't know whether this would make a piece but I think even you would be surprised. Why don't you give us a buzz and drop in? We could put you up at a special price.'

When I arrived at Noshleigh station there were two cabs on the rank, but neither of the drivers had ever heard of Hardtack Hall. I showed them the brochure. 'That's the old Asylum in Hardtack Lane,' said one. 'They say it's going to be a hotel. Happen whoever's pouring money into that would *need* to be insane.'

As we drove through the gates I noticed a hastily painted sign which read 'Hardtack Hall. Listed Building. Opening as a Country House Hotel this Easter.' And then rather desperately in more recent paint had been added 'Book Now to avoid disappointment'.

'And bring your own straitjacket,' said the taxi driver laughing mirthlessly. 'That'll be £4.' As he reversed round the asphalt the front door opened and there stood Gunge in a loud check suit reminiscent of the kind of clothing sported by Lord Emsworth of Blandings Castle.

'Ah, dear boy,' he boomed, 'glad you could make it. Come you in.' Gunge deposited his shooting stick in an iron umbrella stand, took off his crofter's tweed hat which was festooned with trout flies, and grasped my hand.

'You are in,' he said, 'right at the start of what could be something quite memorable. Mrs Gunge and I are in the process of restoring dear old Hardtack Hall to its former glory and only just in the nick of time. The council had put a demolition order on it. A very flawed decision that would have been. Hardtack Hall goes right back into history; it's part of our irreconcilable heritage.'

I said the taxi driver had told me it had been a lunatic asylum. 'Malicious rubbish,' said Gunge dismissively. 'I think there might have been some medical use during the Great War when Sir Josiah Hardtack and his sons were decimated on the Somme, but it has always been a great country house in the noble tradition. Come ye into the billiard room.'

Gunge's voice was beginning to sound more and more like C. Aubrey Smith playing little Lord Fauntleroy's grandfather, and he had surreptitiously slipped a monocle into his left eye. 'In its way,' he said, 'Hardtack is as historic a house as Longleat, Hatfield or Cliveden. Though, naturally, on a smaller more intimate scale.'

He said they were lucky to get it cheap because they had spent a packet on it. 'We are going for the American market; in fact we thought of changing the name to Hardtack Castle – they love a castle, the

Yanks, I mean look at the way they flock to Inverlochy and such like, but I think we've got it just about right. Anyway "Hall" has a nice Norman ring doesn't it?'

Gunge explained at great length that he had a theory that there had been an earlier building on the site before Sir Josiah Hardtack had erected the present edifice. 'He was very much the philanthrope, Derrick. The Hardtacks were ironmasters, loomwrights, machinists, men of substance. And yet Sir Josiah's grandfather went to the mill at dawn every morning of the year in his clogs and expected his workforce of 2,000 to follow suit.'

Gunge told me that the new hotel had been financed with the help of Sir Toby Gladbladder and a group of his friends who were used to taking a gamble. 'Commodity brokers, developers, men of substance,' said Gunge, 'but they have left all the domestic details to Mrs Gunge and myself. We went on a very extensive tour looking at places like Gravetye Manor, Cromlix, Stoneaston, all these places which are doing well. Now they've each got a little bit the others haven't got. But none of them have got it all in *one* place. That's really going to be the secret of Hardtack Hall. Once you've stayed here you won't want to go anywhere else.'

Every room, Gunge explained, would have a four-poster bed and its own personal suit of armour, simulated Flemish tapestry, olde oak chest and trouser press.

'We shall have peacocks, Highland cattle and Père David deer on the lawns and each of the public

rooms has got its own little theme.'

At that moment Mrs Gunge came down the main staircase in a striking Nell Gwyn outfit, her hair raised in a beehive pompadour.

'Isn't she a picture, a perfect hostess for a perfect house. Just the person to give you a guided tour because her delicate hand has been at work in every room.'

Thora blushed prettily and led us into the dining-room which was papered in artery-red brushed velvet flock with heavily swagged bottle-green curtains. The carpet was in matching textured jade of eclectic pattern.

'Sumptuous, isn't it?' said Thora, looking round with evident pride. 'A little touch of the Trianon and a suggestion of Versailles, I feel, and really atmospheric when we light the medieval gas-log fire and lower the Ever-glo baroque flambeaux.'

Pink napkins on the brick-red tablecloths and the chairs button-backed in simulated blue leatherette all added to the busy feel of the room.

'It's here,' said Gunge, 'that Chef's finest creations will be displayed.' It was the mark of a good country house hotel, Gunge explained, to have a young English chef who had done his time in the great kitchens of Europe.

'A very good training ground,' I agreed.

'Yes, young John's a protégé of the Foie Gras brothers.'

'You mean he cooked with Jean-Pierre, Jean-Claude, Alain, Raoul and Yves, the celebrated chef-patrons of the Dordogne?'

'Not *cooked* with them, washed up for them!'

Gunge said that young John in a meteoric career had been a trainee *plongeur* with Michel Roux at the Waterside, Raymond Blanc at the Quat' Saisons, Pierre Koffman at Tante Claire and Nico Ladenis at Shinfield.

'Wonderful experience, and of course we're bringing him on here gradually. But he's got it all at his fingertips – *cuisine nouvelle, naturelle, unnaturelle*, he's washed it all up.'

It was too early, Gunge thought, for Michelin stars but they would inevitably come once the quality of the cuisine became apparent.

'I shall continue to flambé on special occasions but this is very much a retirement venture for Mrs Gunge and myself. Enabling others to enjoy the pleasures of yesteryear in truly splendid surroundings.'

The bedrooms in Hardtack Hall were a skilful blend of modern styling and country chintz. Indeed there was little not upholstered in lavender chintz, including lavatory seats which all bore a paper riband bearing the legend 'sanitised for your convenience'. All the rooms had personal scenarios which Thora herself had thought thoughtfully through.

'This is the crinoline lady room,' said Thora, opening a door on to a vision of figurines and gewgaws all exploiting this interesting theme.

'I love crinoline,' said Thora, showing me the bathroom in which even the spare bog roll had been chastely concealed beneath a knitted crinolined cosy.

She caught me peering closely at the pictures which seemed to be varnished photographs of paintings depicting cardinals carousing at table, smiths shoeing horses under spreading chestnut trees, sheep in snow, rotund monks getting drunk in monastery cellars, and ships under full and fatal sail foundering on rocky shores.

'You're admiring our art treasures,' said Thora, brightening. 'All these are genuine reproductions. They're washable but have a Varnitex finish to give that authentic look. *I'm* very pleased with them too.'

She told me that I would love the library and led us down a long corridor to a bleak room with a TV set and little else.

'This is coming on, I think,' said Gunge. 'We're not quite there yet, but you get the general idea.'

'There are no books,' I said.

'Books get very dusty,' said Thora, 'we shall have lots of nice mags. We shall have a full range just like you find in any country house – *Rod and Feather*, *Cleaning Antiques*, *Gracious Living*, *Country Things*, *Country Life*, *Country Gardens*, and *Killing Animals*.'

Over a pot of tea for three brought in by a person dressed as an undertaker Gunge discoursed on his philosophy of the country house hotel.

'Now you saw the lad who brought the tea. A pity he dropped the Kunzle cakes but bear with him, we're all learning at this stage. Now he's not a waiter, he's a footman, an under footman. Above him is a steward and above him a butler. These sort of places always had a butler.'

Gunge went on to explain that they were selling a

dream. 'A dream of grandeur. *Upstairs Downstairs* brought to life before your very eyes, for large sums of money, of course. I mean, we've got to live.'

It was for the American market that Gunge and his co-directors had gone. 'They've got no history themselves so we sell it to them by proxy. You'll notice the Jacobean armchairs, the Elizabethan cocktail cabinet, the Restoration coats of arms on the Lords and Ladies. I'm not saying those belonged to the Hardtacks, but they are very much a part of the sort of background this sort of place had or should have – if you follow me.'

Gunge wiped his monocle, screwed it in his eye and winked. 'A hotel is theatre,' he boomed in the ripe tones of Donald Sinden, 'giving people a feel of a golden age which they have never enjoyed. But why not? As Field Marshal McLuhan said, and I never tire of quoting that wonderful old sage, "history is bunk – make your own!" '

In the months to come there would be a full employment of marketing tools – wine seminars, flower arranging, cookery courses, vintage car rallies, music weekends, and guest appearances by celebrities like Jimmy Young and Little and Large.

'It needs time to get it right. You can't hurry history. But mother and I have got plenty of time now we're in the autumn of our lives. We shall enjoy living here and entertaining people with more money than sense.'

Gunge lit a large cigar and waved it expansively in the air. 'It's all tax-deductible, isn't it?'

Thora laughed uneasily. 'You'll be giving Mr

Cooper the wrong idea.'

'How long have you known me, Derrick?'

'Well,' I said, 'it must be twenty years or more.'

'Right. And have I ever put a foot wrong? We're still out in the forefront, Derrick – we always have been and we always will. Have a glass of bubbly?'

As Gunge rose and rang a large brass handbell a limousine drew up at the front door.

'Ooh,' said Thora, brightening, 'visitors!'

A couple festooned with cameras and clad in cashmere and Burberries stood hesitantly on the doorstep.

'We're the Waffenbeckers from Spittoon, Ohio,' said the man. 'We're on our way to stay at Miller Howe and we read about your place in the *New York Times*. This *is* Hardtack Hall?'

'Why bless you, yes!' said Gunge.

'And you must be Lord. . .?'

'Lord love you to be sure,' boomed Gunge, 'welcome to Hardtack Hall, noblest old pile of the North.'

'Would you have a room for the night?'

'Room, sir, we have a whole wing at your disposal. Thora, ask our chatelaine to show these very wonderful people to the Lady Hardtack suite with private facilities and south-facing balcony, £280 a night with hearty English breakfast.'

A girl who looked uncannily like Doris the cashier from the Café Royal began sorting out the huge pile of Gucci luggage which the chauffeur was assembling from the Mercedes.

'If you'll follow me, Mr and Mrs Waffenbecker,'

gushed Thora, 'I'll guide you to your apartments.'

'You see,' said Gunge as the Americans disappeared along an upper corridor, 'it's all happening, isn't it? Ah, the champers.' Gunge unwrapped the foil on a bottle of Asti Spumante *dolce* and poured three foaming glasses. 'Cheers. There's nothing like Pol Roger is there? Did you know it was Winnie's favourite champagne? They say the old boy stayed here during the war – with their Majesties of course and the royal kiddies.'

I could see a misty look come into Gunge's eyes.

'You know, Derrick,' he said, 'it's a wonderful country this olde England of ours.'

It could have been the smoke from his cheroot, or perhaps genuine emotion, but there was moisture in Gunge's eyes. Then bravely he pulled himself together.

'Time,' he said, 'to dress for dinner. The kilt I think tonight. We always have a Highland evening on Tuesdays. Might ask the Waffenbeckers to sit at High Table with us, they look harmless enough. You'll find your own way back to the station, won't you Derrick, and keep in touch, dear boy.'

Gunge drained his glass and made his way up the grand staircase. At the top he paused under a pair of outsize antlers and raised a farewell hand.

'Haste ye back,' he cried, 'and have a good day!'

I rang the handbell softly and Doris brought my coat. With it there was a bill for £18.50 for champagne.

There was never anyone quite like Gunge.